PRAISE FOR AK TURNER

"Another hilarious account of parenthood . . . With her characteristic good-spirited, self-deprecating humor, Turner describes taking her kids to a children's art camp on the Jersey Shore and surviving a back-to-school night 'ice cream unsocial.' Well paced, entertaining, and full of endearing stories on parenting, this new addition to Turner's popular series will leave readers looking forward to the next installment."

—*Publishers Weekly* Starred Review of *Hair of the Corn Dog*

"AK Turner is *always* funny."

—Jen Mann, *New York Times* bestselling author of *People I Want to Punch in the Throat*

"It's rare for a writer to actually make me laugh out loud, but AK Turner does just that."

—Robin O'Bryant, *New York Times* bestselling author of *Ketchup Is a Vegetable and Other Lies Moms Tell Themselves*

"I laughed out loud at *Mommy Had a Little Flask,* but make no mistake, this book is equally heartfelt and humorous as AK Turner delves into all the wonders, challenges and horrifying playground moments of parenting— the most extreme sport there is."

—Cameron Morfit, *Sports Illustrated*

"AK Turner's writing manages to be both hilarious and heartfelt at the same time. When I read her words, I find myself laughing to the point of tears one minute and then crying real tears the next. It's writing that makes you feel something. Something real and deep and honest. Which is how writing should be."

—Deva Dalporto, *MyLifeSuckers*

"AK Turner is the best friend that we dream of having: smart, eloquent, and she doesn't take herself too seriously. You can't help but envision yourself right alongside of her, cheering, laughing, and thanking your lucky stars that you have her in your life."

—Lynn Morrison, *The Nomad Mom Diary*

"The thing that I can't get over with AK Turner is that she is endlessly fresh. Funny, always, but fresh, sweet funny that keeps me coming back again and again . . . and craving more. Always can't wait to read her latest."

—Meredith Spidel, *The Mom of the Year*

Vagabonding

with kids

Vagabonding
with kids

AK TURNER

BROWN BOOKS
PUBLISHING GROUP

Vagabonding with Kids

Brown Books Publishing Group
16250 Knoll Trail Drive, Suite 205
Dallas, Texas 75248
www.BrownBooks.com
(972) 381-0009
A New Era in Publishing®

ISBN 978-1-61254-914-9
LCCN 2016937101

Printed in the United States
10 9 8 7 6 5 4 3 2 1

Design by Sarah Tregay, DesignWorks Creative, Inc.
Cover photos by Amaura Mitchell and iStock
Author photo by Mike Turner

For more information or to contact the author, please go to VagabondingWithKids.com or AKTurner.com.

For my mother, who led me to believe that standing still was far more dangerous than exploring the world.

She was right.

CONTENTS

Introduction

There's no denying that travel is uncomfortable. And really, what's better than comfort? Why would anyone invite a state of *dis*comfort? It makes no sense. We should cuddle up on the couch with a blanket and beverage, ready to binge on an entire season of guilty pleasures on Netflix, something in which ridiculously attractive people repeatedly engage in horrific behavior. Getting comfy and watching the misfortunes of others is a great American pastime.

Exploring the world is the opposite of staying comfortable. Think of Ernest Shackleton or the Lewis and Clark expeditions or surviving an extended layover at LAX. The last thing that comes to mind is comfort. Instead, "exploring" conjures up images of frostbite, inadequate plumbing, and what will happen when you inexplicably blurt "Bomb!" while going through security. Or maybe that's just me.

Experience tells me that travel includes unexpected extreme temperatures, sleeping in uncomfortable places and positions, and potential havoc on my digestive tract. And what if that havoc grew to such an extent that I'd have to visit foreign doctors in foreign lands? Would they even know what they were doing? What other ailments, worse than my original complaint, would I acquire after seeking help? How soon might a bout of Montezuma's revenge be nothing in comparison to the malaria I've now contracted? Or worse, I'd be involved in a case of mistaken identity and wake up having undergone a completely unnecessary amputation. Meanwhile, the guy in the hall with the gangrenous leg would be wondering why all they'd done was ply him with Alka-Seltzer.

If a disastrous trip abroad doesn't sound nightmarish enough, you could always take it to the next level with vagabonding. Definitions of vagabond vary, from "disreputable" and "worthless" to "wandering from place to place without a settled home; nomadic." In the world of digital nomads—also known as people who work primarily via their laptops and can therefore operate from anywhere in the world that has a semi-dependable Internet connection—vagabonding is generally looked at as living and working in foreign locations for months at a time on a limited budget. It's perfect when you want to take the discomfort of travel and stretch it for an entire season or more.

As a concept, vagabonding is logistically difficult for those of us raised to covet a house, a car, job stability, and a retirement fund. How could I reconcile paying rent or a mortgage on a residence that I'd leave vacant for months on end? If I rid myself of the permanent address, where would I put my belongings? If I kept my home, who would water my plants and collect my mail? Who would make sure my pipes didn't freeze and squatters didn't move in to deal drugs out of my garage? I couldn't let anyone else stay in my house because they'd see my *things*. They might even use my things and break my things. *My* things. What if they wore my underwear or did nasty things on my bed? I'd have to take all of my underwear with me to make sure that didn't happen, but that would occupy valuable real estate in my luggage. All of this is problematic for the average control freak like me, because when you leave your surroundings, you can no longer control them.

Despite these challenges, my husband, Mike, and I fell into a state of vagabonding in our twenties. This is the one time in life when others view vagabonding as borderline acceptable, though still indicative of a slightly subversive lifestyle. We didn't set out to vagabond, nor did we recognize it as such, but three months in London led to three months in Morocco, followed by similar stints in Spain, the South Pacific, and Micronesia. One day we realized it had been two years since we'd lived anywhere one might describe as *home*.

When we started a family, the idea of vagabonding, romanticized and reserved for the young and childless, became incandescently troublesome. It would be one thing to expose myself to the dangers beyond my front door but quite another to put my children at risk. The earth teemed with toxic spiders, flesh-eating bacteria, and bad people. Motherhood wasn't supposed to include any of those things. So when I became a parent, I shed the notion of vagabonding, mentally replacing Thailand with CandyLand and suitcases with diaper bags. I'd be content to live in one place year-round to provide a consistent and stable environment in which my children would thrive. I'd embrace domesticity and Pinterest fails, and we'd adapt to an annual, two-week family vacation, likely to a large and expensive theme park where my husband would struggle to suppress his irrational panic attacks when being made to wait in line, and I'd worry about people in animal costumes dropping dead from heat exhaustion.

The trips we would take would have to be confined to school breaks, because I couldn't compromise my children's attendance. How would I explain a vagabonding scenario to school administrators? I could lie, of course, and claim that top-secret government work required me to temporarily relocate my family to a location that I was not at liberty to disclose. But I don't come close to looking like I might be that important. And their education would be the priority, anyway. If they fell behind in kindergarten, which they would, because I was not a licensed educator and therefore surely couldn't teach the A-B-Cs and 1-2-3s, their delays would carry through and compound year after year. They'd be held back more than once. I'd be lucky if they even graduated. Beyond that, the damage I'd do to my children socially by interrupting the school year would be downright cruel. Their truancy would result in lost friends and depression. They'd be taunted, ridiculed, and given monikers like Dirty Hippie Gypsy Kid. And it would be my fault. If we continued to vagabond, I'd be a horrible parent.

I've never been independently wealthy. Nor have I been *dependently* wealthy; no overly indulgent and grossly rich relative has offered to finance my jaunting about the globe. Mike and I have lived through good years and almost-made-it-above-the-poverty-line years. Through all of the years, we've carried debt. I've never aspired to surmount the debt, just to coexist with it. The fact that we've never been financially rich was yet another reason to exclude extended travel as a logical possibility. Airline tickets are expensive. Hotels are expensive. Heck, even *tents* are expensive. Rental cars, baggage fees, visas, and insurance are expensive. Everything is expensive. And that's not even accounting for all the expensive unexpected expenses. If we were going to travel after becoming parents, I reasoned, it would be wise to delay it for the day when all of our existing debt was paid off, whether or not that day ever occurred. And travel would best be relegated to the later years anyway, to serve as an occupying distraction when we'd be empty-nesters and retirees. In the golden years, we'd have all the time in the world to travel.

For our family of four, the timing would never be right. There was school to consider. Travel was too expensive. Vagabonding was dangerous, dirty, and logistically baffling. There were a million reasons not to travel, countless ways to talk ourselves out of exploring the world.

The problem was none of them were true. Letting fear hold us back from invaluable cultural experiences would be an easy way of living but not necessarily a better one.

To date, Mike and I have visited more than two dozen countries around the world, often staying for months at a time. Half of those adventures have taken place since starting a family and included our daughters, Ivy and Emilia, ages seven and nine at present. The stories that follow chronicle the mistakes we've made, the fears we've conquered and the ones we're still working on, and the unexpected rewards that emerge when an average American family embraces an uncommon approach to life.

* * *

Becoming Vagabonds

Vagabonding is not a lifestyle, nor is it a trend.
It's just an uncommon way of looking at life—
a value adjustment from which action naturally follows.

—Rolf Potts, *Vagabonding*

"I'm sorry, but her eyes have to be open," the clerk said. I was in a drugstore attempting to have Emilia's passport photo taken. She was two weeks old.

"Come on, baby," I said, jiggling and prodding her to return to consciousness while propping her upright but trying to stay out of the shot myself. This required holding ten squishy, sleeping pounds up over my head and away from body, which is no easy feat. My arms strained, and my armpits began to sweat. Was that moisture I felt, seeping from her diaper? Would a stream of urine (or worse) begin snaking its way down my arm? *Everything will be okay,* I told myself, *as long as you don't drop the baby.*

The clerk smiled nervously, caught between amusement at the situation and what looked like suspicion, as if procuring a passport for a newborn indicated nefarious purposes on my part. Perhaps I was trying to kidnap the child or exploiting her to gain inside knowledge for a business in passport counterfeiting. Whatever his concerns, he put them aside. It took five minutes until he was able to snap a photo during a weak flutter of eyelids.

Just a few years before, I looked at travelers with small children with a similar curiosity. There could be no good reason for taking a child on a plane all the way from Los Angeles to Sydney, Australia, for instance. And as we made that flight, childless and for the first time, I assumed that all of my fellow travelers with children must be in the process of moving their permanent residence from the United States to Australia, because I could see no other motive that would make such an undertaking of fifteen hours on a plane with a child worth it.

"Mike?" I pretended not to notice that my husband was sleeping during the aforementioned flight and elbowed him awake.

"Yeah?"

"Did you know that when we get to Sydney, we have a fourteen-hour layover?"

"Yeah," he mumbled.

"What are we going to do for fourteen hours?"

"We'll go see the, you know, the stuff there."

"The stuff there?"

"Yeah, the stuff that's there to see, we'll go see that."

"Yes, but fourteen hours? We might have to rent a room or something."

This perked him up, as if my motivation for renting a room had to do with anything other than a solid nap.

"Seriously, Mike, fourteen hours is a long time. What are we going to do with ourselves?"

"Don't worry, Amanda," he assured me, "we'll tackle that stone when we cross it."

I let him drift back to sleep while I pondered the combination of words he'd put together and pictured him determinedly wrestling a series of immovable boulders.

When we reached Sydney, we paid a baggage service to secure our luggage while we ventured out of the airport. In other words, we handed over cash for someone to take our suitcases into a private room, rifle through them, and pocket our valuables. We would later find that a Leatherman tool I'd bought Mike for his birthday was missing, and in return we ended up with someone else's toiletry bag. When I discovered the bag, I was sure it would have wildly exciting contents, like drugs, a roll of hundred-dollar bills, and a revolver. But the toiletry bag was disappointingly filled with toiletries. Not only are a stranger's nail clippers and razors less than dramatic but also a bit gross.

Unaware of the theft that was occurring, we took a train to the Circular Quay, window-shopped, strolled around the harbor, and eventually made our way to a park bench, whose hard, wooden slats beckoned to us. It wasn't as comfortable as the hotel room about which my husband and I had very different fantasies, but it was free. We napped on and off for the remaining hours of our monstrous layover until making our way back to the airport for the final leg of our journey. Our destination was a Y-shaped archipelago of more than eighty small islands in the South Pacific known as Vanuatu. We were headed for the capital city of Port Vila on the island of Efate.

The previous year saw us living in England, Morocco, and Spain, with smaller side trips to Italy, Greece, France, the Czech Republic, and Mexico. We'd fallen into the nomadic lifestyle by chance. After college, Mike landed what was supposed to be a dream job. It paid well and came with a company car. Living on ramen noodles and struggling to make rent payments for years came to an end, and the combination of money, wheels, and a gas station credit card seemed like answered prayers. But in the year that followed, I watched my husband's elation give way to encroaching resentment. The commute was brutal, the work was depressing, and the hours never ended. When his first annual review approached, a small spark came back into his eyes.

"I know what I'm going to say at my review," he announced. "They're going to offer me a raise, but I'm going to tell them I don't want a raise."

"Wait, you don't want a raise?"

"No. I want more time off. I'm going to ask for an extra week of vacation time instead."

The day of his review, he came home more depressed than ever. "Did you get the extra week of vacation time?" I asked, though his demeanor told me the answer.

"No," he said. "They said no. They gave me a raise." I hadn't thought it possible for someone to look so sad while communicating that he'd received a pay increase.

Mike settled into a state of dissatisfaction and routine. And then he received the phone call that would rearrange our lives. A friend from college wanted to employ my husband in the movie business, and it would require us to live and work at different film locations around the world. He gleefully quit the corporate dream job, and in the fifteen years since, he has not once lamented the loss of money or job stability.

As Air Vanuatu carried us closer to tropical forests and active volcanoes, I pressed my head to the window.

"It looks pretty amazing," I said to Mike.

"It looks *awesome*," he agreed.

The plane began a slight descent, and a baby howled. The mother tried to shush and rock her child back into complacency, to no avail. Minutes went by, and the air grew tense as passengers waited for silence. We glanced at the mother with a combination of sympathy, pity, and annoyance. The crying increased. The mother unbuckled her seat belt to stand so that she might better rock the baby, but a flight attendant quickly instructed her to sit back down.

"We are not doing that," I said.

"Doing what?" Mike asked.

"Taking kids on long trips."

"Hell no," he agreed. "That sounds like a terrible idea."

"We'd never get first-class upgrades."

"We couldn't drink in airport bars."

"And that's the only thing that makes airports redeemable," I said.

"We'll travel with our kids when they're older. Like when they're teenagers."

"If we even *have* kids," I added.

In Port Vila, we disembarked, and a group of locals, clad in matching shirts with bright tropical prints, welcomed us on the runway, singing and playing ukuleles. Vanuatu is an endearing place to be, where the language has a lilting cadence and everyone carries a machete. To this day, I believe the Ni-Van to be the friendliest people on earth. I spent my three months there making endless trips from one side of Efate to the other in a beat-up pickup truck, into which I welcomed many a machete-wielding stranger who might otherwise spend hours hacking his way through the jungle in an effort to get home to his family after a long day of work. On many occasions, the people I offered rides to declined, explaining that they were not going to or from work but rather training for an annual race that leads runners on a series of roads circling the island. At least half of the competitors I witnessed, either in training or on the day of the race, ran barefoot. Others donned flip-flops, and a select few sported sneakers. The surface underneath them changed from hard-packed dirt to pavement to loose gravel, and the runners, of both sexes and varying ages, never seemed to notice. I can't walk to my mailbox barefoot. Eventually I learned to spot runners as opposed to commuters, because long-distance runners were never armed with machetes. As a result, I learned to offer rides only to machete-wielding strangers.

My job in Vanuatu involved scouring the island for hardware needed at the work site, which is more difficult than it sounds with nary a Home Depot to be found. I also ran errands and drove other employees to various locations. Pigs were as common as machetes and just as valuable. One of the locals with whom we worked desperately wanted to marry his girlfriend but explained that he did not yet have enough pigs to present to his would-be father-in-law. One day, I drove yet another local worker, John Bosco, to his home in the Black Sands village. John Bosco was a gem. Hardworking, intelligent, and a genuinely nice man, he was skilled in more areas than anyone I've ever known. Not only had he mastered a multitude of trades like welding and carpentry, but he was also known to emerge from the jungle having caught, bare-handed, a pair of wild chickens.

"Amanda," he said when we neared his home, "do you want to meet Bull Mackau?"

"Um, okay," I replied, not knowing who Bull Mackau was but feeling like I should.

"Wait until you see Bull Mackau." John Bosco smiled. "I think you will like him."

In a large pen, littered with trash and debris, lived a giant pig. He reminded me, size-wise, of a Volkswagen I'd once owned. I approached the beast, who seemed to be weighing in his mind how much he wanted to move away from me versus how much energy the act would require.

"Normally we raise the pigs and then eat them," John Bosco explained, "but Bull Mackau got so fat that now he is too much fat and not enough meat. So now he is our pet." This is the only time in my life when I encountered a creature whose obesity was beneficial.

"Hi," I whispered to Bull Mackau and crouched closer. He grunted and lifted to his front hooves, though it looked like lifting to his hind legs as well would be too much for him. "It's okay," I said. We stared at each other for a minute or so before I left. I wanted to stay and scratch his belly and make him love me, but I only made him uncomfortable, I could tell, so I retreated slowly. Meeting Bull Mackau was one of those strange moments in life when staring into the eyes of a five-hundred-pound swine on a volcanic archipelago in the South Pacific makes you understand that exploring the world isn't something you want to outgrow—ever.

* * *

Our two years around the world came to an end. We settled into a home and self-employment in Idaho, traveling whenever we could but on a smaller scale. As we inched ever closer to parenthood, people told us about all the things we would have to give up once we had a child, travel being chief among them. I thought often of the mother and her crying baby en route from Sydney to Vanuatu. The flight had been uncomfortable, surely for the mother more than anyone else, but aren't all flights uncomfortable? As long as the plane lands, I consider the flight a success. Perhaps we'd travel differently with children, but I didn't think giving it up entirely was possible.

Our trips with children were limited at first. We tackled the procurement of passports for a newborn who refused to open her eyes on command and quickly moved on to the challenges of changing a soiled diaper on the floor of a commuter plane. The extent to which the diaper was soiled determined whether or not we referred to the event as a "Code Yellow" or the much more dreaded "Code Brown." Those were uncomfortable situations but nothing that merited forgoing a trip.

We learned that jet lag isn't a problem for babies, who are accustomed to periodic napping and overcome even the most drastic of time changes in a mere twenty-four hours. We found ourselves paying extortionist rates for packs of baby wipes in rural areas but always with gratitude that baby wipes were available, no matter the price. Traveling with infants and toddlers shaped us into far more adaptable parents than we'd have been if we remained within the familiarity of our hometown.

By the time we shed strollers and diaper bags, it became clear that our children were not only capable when it came to travel but also benefited from it. Before a two-month trip to Australia, Emilia (who'd long since outgrown her sleepy-newborn passport) struggled to make friends in her second-grade class. She had an awkward and tentative approach when it came to interacting with her peers. During our time abroad, she developed confidence, inquisitiveness, and unrestrained kindness. And upon her return to second grade in the United States, she regaled her classmates with tales of kangaroos and her dramatic survival of a jellyfish sting. Her awkwardness, for which I claim full responsibility, may remain in part, but there is nothing tentative about her.

Our children were more adaptable and accepting than we'd given them credit for. They made friends the world over, learning that language barriers are easily overcome with smiles and imagination. They emerged into travelers who do not balk at fourteen-hour flights and unfamiliar insects. In the absence of toys, they created imaginary worlds where fallen mangos are precious gems to be collected. Without the comforts of home, they found adventure in the most unsavory hotel rooms, drawing treasure maps for each other, forcing the explorer to navigate through towering palm trees (bath towels), around a grumpy troll (mini-fridge), to reach the lost city of rainbows (a bed). Emboldened by their adaptability, which expanded our own willingness to venture, the locations of our trips stretched farther from home, and their durations dominated more of the calendar. By the time our children were three and five, we had eased into a state of part-time vagabonding, committing to living and working in a different country for an average of three months a year. We were unintentional vagabonds before kids, and after a brief respite, our kids proved to us that this approach to life was not only possible for our family of four but also the most appropriate one for us.

Most of the people we encounter show support for (and sometimes envy of) our commitment to extended travel with our children, but occasionally we meet people who assure us that our choices in life are terrible decisions. Each trip we take affirms that it is never wise to pay much attention to those who advise, "You just can't do that; it'll never work." Possibility has nothing to do with convention, and there have been times when I've almost let the latter get in the way of the former or momentarily listened to the naysayers. We're firmly on the other side of those doubts and obstacles now, committed to how we live and move about the world. To many, getting to this point seems like a difficult journey in itself, but for me, making the move to our current life most resembles Emilia struggling for that first passport photo. I just needed to open my eyes.

* * *

How Can We Afford This?

Money often costs too much.
—Ralph Waldo Emerson

For too long, I believed that people who traveled extensively were either paid to do so, were spending a long-saved retirement fund, or were millionaires. Mike was patient in his efforts to convince me that this needn't be the case, but it wasn't easy. Our pre-kid travels had been work-related, so our employer paid for airline tickets and accommodations. But the prospect of traveling as a self-employed family meant the costs landed in our laps. Over time, I've relaxed my attitude about the price tag of travel, while we've simultaneously found ways to soften its impact.

Airline miles don't provide an endless supply of free plane tickets, but every now and then, they do add up. This is especially important when you make the bittersweet transition from having a child who travels for free, but must do so on your lap, to having a child whose seat is just as expensive as your own. The shock of having to pay for four tickets instead of two is jarring.

"I feel like now we can't afford to go anywhere," I said when Ivy turned two and could therefore no longer travel for free.

"Just think of every time we've been on a plane when you've had a kid on your lap," Mike said.

"What's your point?"

"Most of those times, you would have begged to hand over your credit card in exchange for an extra seat."

"Well, that's true," I agreed. "There's nothing worse than a kid on your lap during a long flight when you suddenly realize her diaper is leaking."

"Or when someone is sleeping on you and your arm goes numb, but you don't want to move for fear of waking the beast," Mike added.

"Yes. Or when they offer wine and you have to say 'no thanks' because there's a kid sprawled across your body."

Mike looked at me with skeptical eyes.

"Okay," I confessed. "I've never actually said 'no thanks' to a glass of wine."

I love my daughters and have loved them both at every age. But when they were squirming, sticky, soggy eighteen-month-olds, I wanted to love them from the comfort of my own, unshared seat and with the benefit of an armrest in between us.

"I'm signing the girls up for their own mileage plans," Mike mentioned.

"You can do that?" This seemed wrong, the equivalent of giving a child a credit card or letting her choose her own outfit to attend a funeral.

"Of course," he said. "Their seats are paid for now, so they earn miles for travel just like we do."

This is an example of when two minds are more useful than one. Getting the children their own mileage numbers would never have occurred to me as a possibility, yet doing so increased our ability to earn miles and cash them in for future travel. Beyond that, we directed small monthly bills to hit the credit card associated with our mileage plan. This is a great idea as long as one is responsible enough not to use it as a path to financial ruin. Getting airline miles for cheaper travel isn't worth much if you've let utility bills pile up on your credit card, the interest rates of which will eventually cost you far more than a plane ticket would have.

Other strategies, like renting out our home or arranging home and vehicle exchanges, have also offset the financial strain. In Australia, we discovered that using a service like DriveMyCar.com.au, which matches would-be renters up with people who have a second, rarely used car and a need for cash, was far cheaper than if we'd approached a typical car rental service. We used DriveMyCar.com.au twice during our trip. One car was a dream, and the other a monumental piece of shit, but it was a very *economical* monumental piece of shit.

The tricks we use to make extended travel financially possible have been learned over time and often the hard way. For every aspect of vagabonding that we have figured out, we've made a series of missteps to get there.

Before working in Micronesia, Mike and I each purchased a set of terribly expensive and incredibly unflattering rain gear. It's the type of clothing that folds up into the size of one square inch and fits into a coordinated, drawstring pouch. I'm a sucker for anything that comes with a drawstring pouch. For the first two weeks of work in Palau, I dutifully carried my rain gear with me at all times, ready for a torrential downpour, the kind that inspires ark builders to snap into action. In all my anal-retentive glory, I vowed to be the prepared one, to whom everyone else would look with envy, wishing they had their own ridiculously overpriced and unattractive rain gear at the ready.

During those first two weeks, the ground grew parched and increasingly dusty with each rain-free passing day. On the fifteenth working day in Palau, I relented in my preparedness by leaving my rain gear at the office while walking around the job site. That was the day the heavens fell. It wasn't as though rain began to drip down from the clouds but more like the air, without warning, turned to liquid. All work ceased, and the crew took refuge under various shelters, some of us more amazed at the deluge than others, depending on our geographic origins. I huddled with my coworkers under a propped-up tarp. I *really* wanted to put my exorbitantly priced rain gear to use. This was the perfect opportunity; this was what I had been waiting for.

In a moment unrepresentative of my best judgment, I dashed back to the office. With each step, my socks and sneakers worked closer to soaking through completely; by the time I reached the office, I squished when I walked. My hair was pasted unattractively to my head, and my clothes stuck to my skin in a manner some might call obscene. I cheerfully greeted those working in the office, ignoring my saturated state. *No matter,* I thought, *since I can now don my brand-new, ultralightweight, super-fancy rain gear.* The pants were brown, and the jacket purple, not necessarily the most flattering combination of colors on me but better than, say, a hot pink and yellow ensemble. Once I had the rain gear on, I began to sweat on a level I never imagined possible. As the perspiration contributed to my moisturized condition, seeping from my pores at turbo speed, the sun came out. The rain tapered off and then stopped completely as I exited the office to find a brilliant sky. At this point, I began to sweat with even more resolve. There was no water for my rain gear to repel from the outside but plenty to keep in. I felt like a baked potato wrapped in foil, and it is also possible that I actually began to steam.

"Nice rain gear, Amanda," I heard as I passed the construction area. I turned to see Martha, one of my few female coworkers, smirking in my direction. Martha was never one to let such an opportunity pass without comment.

"Thanks," I answered.

"It's not raining anymore, you know."

"I know. It's just really comfortable. And besides, it could rain again any time." Martha and I looked up at the clear blue sky, from which the rain clouds had sprinted.

"You sure you're all right? You look a little red."

"No, I'm cool." In fact, I thought I might pass out at any moment, and when I looked in a mirror later, I found that I was not merely a bit flushed but that my face looked like a large, red tomato.

There was no doubt that the rain gear was high quality, but it was not intended for a tropical climate. And my insistence on wearing it stemmed from the unacknowledged truth that I'd spent a lot of money on something I didn't need. One mistaken purchase might not seem like a big deal, but it's never just one. In advance of a trip, an otherwise rational and financially responsible individual will convince himself that he needs new luggage, backpacks, hiking boots, and thermal underwear, despite the fact that he already owns perfectly good luggage, backpacks, hiking boots, and thermal underwear. And while "new" might seem better, it rarely is, because now the traveler finds himself in unfamiliar land with unfamiliar gear, pining for the comfort of his well-worn (but perfectly good) thermal underwear and boots at home. Then there are gadgets and knickknacks. When shopping for the new but unnecessary backpack, the traveler is presented with a million other unnecessary items, like soap holders and toothbrush holders and razor holders, which he will stuff into his new backpack (also known as a stuff holder).

My experiences taught me that if we were truly going to travel long term, I needed to rid myself of the compulsion to get an REI credit card every time we added a leg to our itinerary.

* * *

"I have some clients I think we should get together with sometime," Mike mentioned one afternoon at our home in Boise. "Maybe we can find a time that works, get a babysitter, and go out to dinner."

"Are we getting a babysitter?" Emilia asked with wide, hopeful eyes.

"Yes, at some point, you'll have a babysitter," Mike answered. "But we're still planning this. We don't know exactly when."

"Yes!" Ivy jumped up and down. "I love babysitters!"

"And that means we'll probably get to eat pizza and play games and watch movies," Emilia said.

"Babysitters are the best people in the world," Ivy added.

"They are *so* nice," Emilia agreed.

I was thankful that this exchange took place within our home and without spectators. Anyone hearing the conversation might suspect Mike and me of systematic cruelty, given our daughters' enthusiasm at the prospect of being cared for by an outsider. In truth, we happen to have an outstanding fleet of babysitters.

"Or we could save on the babysitter," I suggested, "and have your clients over for dinner. I *am* a fantastic cook, you know."

"You can't tell us we're going to have a babysitter and then change your mind," Emilia insisted, as if I'd canceled a long-awaited trip to Disneyland.

"Yes, I can," I corrected her.

"Come on, Emilia," Ivy said. "Let's go to our room and play Pretend Babysitter."

"I don't know about having the clients over," Mike said, his voice a higher pitch than usual. He turned his head to the side and scratched the back of his neck.

"What?" I asked.

"I think it's better if we go out to eat."

"Why?"

"I'm not sure I want them to see our house."

"You're ashamed of our house?" I asked, with a brief panic that my domestic skills were under attack. Had I, a near-compulsive cleaner who delights in the smells of Lysol and bleach, lapsed in my self-appointed duties? Had our house become disgusting at a rate slow enough to keep me from recognizing the filth? "Oh my god, just tell me what's disgusting. Do I need to clean something? What's *disgusting?*" I demanded.

"Honey, please don't clean anything. Nothing's disgusting."

"Oh, so it really is just the house you're ashamed of."

"No, I'm not ashamed of our house. I just think they'll be surprised when they see it."

"What's surprising about our house?"

"I think most people assume we're really wealthy. *Really* wealthy."

Our home was built in the late 1950s. It's been upgraded here and there over the years, but you won't find granite or fountains, vaulted ceilings or a theater room. It's not very big, compared to the monstrosities en vogue at the moment, though more than adequate for our family of four. We also drive used cars, eschew five-dollar cups of coffee, and think fine wines are, on more occasions than not, a scam. (Also, when you reach my level of wine consumption, you can't afford the pricey stuff.)

"Why do you think they assume we're rich? Because you own your own brokerage?"

"Maybe that's part of it," he acknowledged, "but it has more to do with how we travel."

When we tell people we're going to live in another country for a few months, not because we've been assigned to do so but because we can and want to, they invariably judge us to be in a higher income bracket than we are.

We went out to dinner with the clients, though I would have been happy to have them over for dinner and shatter any preconceived notions they might have had about who we are and how we live. Mike's apprehension was that if his clients learned that we were less wealthy than they'd thought, that might cast doubts on his business and competence. He would eventually transcend this reluctance.

"You know," he said, "if we didn't travel as much, we'd have more money."

"Ugh," I groaned. "That sounds awful."

Mike agreed.

When we're living on the other side of the world, learning to navigate daily life in an unfamiliar city, language, and culture, we *feel* wealthy. If we didn't travel, we could pad our account a little and have cash to spend on shiny things. In a society that encourages us to covet money for status, money for power, and money for the mere sake of money, it's not easy to recognize that our wealth of positive interactions, family experiences, and sense of adventure is worth more than its monetary counterpart.

Money and gratitude share an imbalanced but symbiotic relationship with regard to prolonged travel. You need both, but just a little of the former and an abundance of the latter. Despite the growing inclination of many to break free from the cubicle and shed the typical nine-to-five with two weeks of vacation per year, many people still assume that the gratitude versus money equation is the other way around.

Plenty of people would disagree with my belief in the importance of gratitude as it relates to travel, including a group of four young Americans who were paired with us on a tour into the Amazon. When we met at the tour office in Manaus, the foursome arrived covered from head to toe in expensive gear, despite the oppressive city heat, and I couldn't help but see a glimpse of myself insisting on overpriced rain gear in Micronesia. From the start, their gear, attitudes, and commentary made it clear that they wanted to leave Brazil having checked Amazon off the list, but that they had no intention of enjoying it along the way. They complained, more than six-year-old Ivy did, of the long walks, bugs, heat, humidity, and lack of hot water.

"I just want to get to Rio and be on the beach where this will all be a distant memory," one of them lamented as soon as we'd completed the half-day's journey, via van, boat, bus, and canoe, from Manaus to the jungle lodge.

"Are we really going to stay here for three full days?" another asked.

"No, dude. No way."

Later that evening, they found a spider in their room and, for fear that the creature might be venomous and attack, they asked our guide to dispatch the arachnid for them. This confirmed the change to their travel plans, and they left the tour early, after one night.

I wondered what they expected to find in the Amazon, if not jungle and all that such a landscape implies. The failure of their experience had nothing to do with a lack of money, as evidenced by their abundance of expensive gear and gadgets. The problem was in their lack of gratitude. They focused more on their discomfort than the wonder of their surroundings. The differences between the jungle lodge and the environments to which they were accustomed were seen as inadequacies, rather than a step into a unique world, one which many people will never have the opportunity to experience. Their reactions to the trip told me that they were used to the ability to go where they wanted, when they wanted, with no consideration of the financial cost. Had they worked for the money to pay for the trip and given careful consideration to how they would use those funds, they likely would have approached the Amazon experience with an open mind, positive outlook, and greater willingness to adapt. Or not. Perhaps they would have bypassed any discomfort and gone straight to Rio. That said, they were young men who may, in time, grow out of their sense of entitlement, and I cannot assert that my behavior at the same age included any greater measure of grace.

When we ask ourselves if we can afford a trip, we give consideration to our level of debt and the general state of our finances, but we also know that while money is important, it won't get us anywhere without greater amounts of gratitude to go along with it. By remaining appreciative of our opportunities and approaching unfamiliar situations with an open mind and kindness, it turns out we can afford far more than we'd thought possible.

* * *

Getting Ready to Go

I still enjoy traveling a lot. I mean, it amazes me that I still get excited in hotel rooms just to see what kind of shampoo they've left me.

—Bill Bryson

Preparing for an extended trip abroad is as exciting as the trip itself, and when children are involved, half the fun is the moment you break the news to your kids of an upcoming adventure. For the past few years, Emilia and Ivy have offered consistent responses when we tell them of future travel plans.

> Me: "Guess what, girls! We have another trip coming up!"
> Emilia: "Ooh, where are we going?"
> Me: "Brazil!" (This is interchangeable with "Bermuda!" "North Dakota!" "Downtown!" "New Jersey!" The location is irrelevant.)
> Emilia: "Yes!" (Clenches fists and eyes while squealing like she hit the jackpot.) "I have *always* wanted to go there!"
> Me: "What do you think, Ivy?"
> Ivy: "Hmm." (Finger to her lips in contemplation, face both serious and suspicious.) "Do they have snacks there?"

While Emilia exudes enthusiasm and begins approaching random strangers to tell them of her travel plans and backstory, Ivy focuses on the one thing she adores.

"Yes, Ivy," I reassure her. "They have snacks in Brazil."

"I think you better bring some, just in case," she warns.

We only inform our children of an upcoming trip when it's a sure thing. Otherwise, it feels like telling them on Christmas morning that you got the date wrong, and Santa's actually not coming for another six weeks. Not that the children aren't as adaptable to changes in plans as they are to new places—even more adaptable than their parents. For instance, if a trip like our impending Brazil adventure were canceled, it's safe to say I'd find myself in a bit of a funk, whereas we could simply tell the girls that Brazil was closed and we were going out for ice cream instead, and they'd accept that as a fair substitute. Still, we typically withhold information until someone has signed or paid for something related to travel, which is a good indication of commitment.

Making that decision, that commitment, is part of the planning process itself and not one that should ever be dragged out, because one of the saddest words I've ever heard is "someday." I've had countless conversations with people who tell Mike and me how lucky we are, as if our expeditions were not conscious decisions but lottery wins instead, and we should squeal and clench our fists like our daughter. And we *are* lucky of course. Poverty and sickness often preclude vagabonding, and we suffer from neither (knock on wood). But the people who tell us how lucky we are don't suffer from poverty or sickness either. They often have more money than we do (though they assume otherwise based on the number of stamps in our passports) and are probably healthier than we are, given my unapologetic and near-constant inclination to open a bottle of wine.

Once we turn "someday" into a concrete date on the calendar, signified by either the purchase of plane tickets or a signed home-exchange agreement, the travel preparations begin. Always first on my list: making sure we can actually get there. If someone's passport is going to expire before our departure (or return) date, well, that's a problem that needs to be addressed. And one should never assume that obtaining or renewing a passport will be a quick and easy task. Obtaining a passport for a minor involves an appointment at a passport office with both parents and the child present, as well as birth certificates, fees, alternate forms of identification, and patience to deal with children and the government at the same time. It requires a fair amount of research and preparation. You cannot simply show up at a passport office and expect to leave with one in half an hour. Weeks, often months, will pass before you have that precious little book in your hand.

Both of my daughters are normal, fairly photogenic children. When posing for a passport photo, however, Emilia has the unfortunate habit of appearing heavily under the influence of marijuana. As a two-week-old baby barely able to keep her eyes open, a bit of a stoned look might be expected, but the same expression plagued her subsequent passport photo. She stood in front of the camera, a bright, blue-eyed, blonde little girl with a wide smile, but just as the camera-wielding drugstore employee pressed the button, her smile turned into a sloppy grimace, and her eyes shifted to a misty half-mast.

"Uh, maybe we'll try one more," said the clerk, this time a middle-aged woman for whom the camera seemed a great challenge.

"Let me take a look," I said, not wanting to make her wrestle with the device more than necessary. When I saw the image of my drugged-out five-year-old on the screen, I had to agree. "Oh, dear. Yes, if we could try that again, that would be great. Thank you."

"Okay, sweetie," said the clerk. "Give me a big smile!"

Once again, Emilia offered clear, shining eyes and a winning smile, which, in the second before the clerk snapped the photo, inexplicably changed into the face of a pothead.

Looking at the image of my daughter, I was reminded of someone I'd known in my teens, an eighteen-year-old who lived in his parents' basement and proudly announced his New Year's resolution to get stoned multiple times a day, every day, for an entire year. "I wake and bake. Then I smoke before work. I smoke on my lunch break. I smoke another bowl after work. Then I smoke a bowl before dinner and one before bed. It's awesome." I didn't know him long enough to find out if he ever achieved his dream.

"Well," the clerk said, trying to muster enthusiasm for the picture, "I guess that one's a little better." To her credit, the clerk tried many times. The important outcome is that my daughter has a valid passport, albeit one that might cause customs officials to suspect her use as a drug mule.

Traveling to Australia required a quick, online visa application and a forty-dollar credit card payment. I stupidly assumed that obtaining a visa for entering Brazil would require similar effort, only to find that the Brazilian consulate requires you to show up in person and hand over original documents like passports and birth certificates, as well as a sizable chunk of money issued on a money order from the United States Postal Service. If you happen not to live near a

Brazilian consulate (we Idahoans are out of luck), then you must employ a service on your behalf, essentially doubling your cost and the time it will take to get that precious little visa in your passport. While some countries require no visa or a very simple process to obtain one, the quest for Brazilian visas (especially when minors are involved) requires high levels of patience and tolerance for redundancy. These documents might seem like a headache, but they are nonnegotiable, so it's best to embrace the process and do so early. The alternative is to bang your head against the wall, but in my experience, doing so will only make the mandatory headache worse.

Vaccinations and medications are nothing to trifle with either—unless you've always been keen to try yellow fever or malaria, but I wouldn't advise it. We tend to think of vaccinations as requiring a quick trip to the doctor and a brief sting of the needle, but many vaccinations require more than one course of the vaccine administered over a set period of time. Exploring your vaccination needs and options is best not left to the week before your trip.

Typhoid vaccinations are administered via a series of pills taken every other day for a week. This becomes problematic with children who have never swallowed pills.

"Let's just see how it goes," Mike said. "I'm sure we can figure it out." We tucked the girls into bed and informed them that before they went to sleep, they each had a pill to swallow.

"You go first, Ivy." I was afraid that if Emilia went first and took the pill with little problem, Ivy would panic and dissolve into a fit of tears, which would only make the task more difficult. "Just put it on the back of your tongue, take a swallow of water, and let the pill slide down with it."

"Okay," she said. She put the pill in her mouth and took a sip of water.

"Did you get it?" I asked. She shook her head. "That's okay. Just try again." She did so with the same result. "Don't worry about it," I assured her. "Just keep trying." And on the third try, without the slightest complaint or protest, she swallowed the pill. "Awesome, Ivy!" Emilia and Mike congratulated her, too, and I felt relief that the pill issue wouldn't be a big deal.

"Now it's your turn, Emilia," Mike said. "Piece of cake."

"Okay." She smiled.

Fifteen minutes and twenty attempts later, the mood had changed. Mike was losing patience, and I knew he was contemplating physically shoving the pill down her throat.

"Just take it, Emilia," he commanded. "The reason it's not working is you're panicking."

"Why do I have to?" she cried. "You guys just go to Brazil for two months without me, and I'll just stay here." She turned to me. "Is that okay?"

Ivy sat silently on her bed. I worried that the pill was dissolving in Emilia's mouth; we'd been given specific instructions to take the pill on an empty stomach so that it made its way to the intestines before absorption.

"Give it to me," Mike demanded, and she spit the soggy pill into his hand. He left the room.

I sat on the edge of her bed, tried to calm her down, and told her again of the importance of guarding ourselves against illnesses we might encounter in other parts of the world. After a few minutes of this, I left to see what Mike was up to. I found him in the kitchen, adding the ground remnants of the pill to a spoonful of yogurt.

"What are you doing? You're not supposed to mix it with food," I said.

"Why not?"

"Just give it to me." I snatched the spoon from his hand, took it to the bedroom where Emilia gulped it down, and returned to the kitchen.

"It's not supposed to be with food?" he asked.

"No, and that's why you take it on an empty stomach. The pill has to get all the way to the intestines before it dissolves."

"Then why'd you take it from me? You shouldn't have given it to her!"

"Because I figured it was better than nothing!"

We continued in this manner for another minute before realizing that there was no point in arguing the matter and that, in all likelihood, no one would be contracting typhoid. Ivy took the remaining pills without issue, and Emilia had one successful attempt, while the others more resembled the first. When the final typhoid pill had been taken, she asked, "How many years is this vaccination good for?"

"Ten," I answered.

She then launched into spontaneous song, the lyrics of which were the repeated proclamation, "No more *pills* for ten more *years*, oh yeah, oh yeah!"

* * *

Mike and I naturally divvy up the preparation tasks into those that best suit us, also known as those about which we care the most. This means that passports, visas, and vaccinations fall on my to-do list, because getting there, being let into the country, and surviving the visit all rank high on my list of vagabonding priorities. Mike's initial research focuses on electronics, Internet, and phone capabilities. He's not interested in gaming, is no Internet junkie, and fails miserably at keeping in phone contact with his friends and relatives. He is, however, a hardworking entrepreneur. For him to enjoy a displaced and foreign state of being for months at a time, he has to remain in fairly steady contact with clients and colleagues. To stay plugged in, he researches any need for adapters and converters, as well as the quality of the Internet connection at our destination. If we're going to stay at a home (through a home exchange) with mediocre Internet, he'll offer to pay for an upgrade of the homeowner's Internet plan before our arrival.

Prior to a month-long trip to Todos Santos, Mexico, Mike contacted our phone provider to see what coverage he would have while south of the border. He was told that his plan worked on the Baja Peninsula. This is half-true. Unfortunately, we would be staying in the other half. While his phone worked well in Cabo San Lucas, he had no coverage when we reached our destination an hour and a half away in Todos Santos. It was a good lesson in preparation, in that we don't always believe what someone in a customer service position tells us and instead try to verify the information with a local. A year later, before returning to Todos Santos for three months of remote working, Mike purchased a prepaid phone from a rival service provider with better coverage, for the specific purpose of making phone calls to clients.

While Mike makes sure he'll be able to communicate with clients back home, I make sure we'll be able to communicate with the locals at our destination. In college, I majored in linguistics with an emphasis in Russian. Over the years, I've dabbled in French, German, Spanish, Czech, and Italian. And when our eldest attended a kindergarten class where half the day was taught in Mandarin Chinese, I demanded she teach me everything she learned, which meant that at one point, both she and I could count quite well in Mandarin Chinese, though by the time she reached second grade, the knowledge was lost. When we travel to non-English-speaking countries, I take the lead on face-to-face communication. Not simply because I have an aptitude for languages but also because my husband and his side of the family are the sort of folk apt to unknowingly use offensive slurs, merge words, create words, or ask you how your autopsy went after a visit to your dermatologist. They mean well and have many skills, but speaking is not their forte.

Conversely, when we travel (and even when we're at home, in the town in which we've lived for over a decade), navigation is relegated to Mike. I lack any semblance of a sense of direction, while my husband moves about the earth as if communicating directly with the sun, moon, and stars.

Six months before heading to Brazil, I began Portuguese lessons with confidence, downloading an audio program, which I looked forward to working through with the children. I envisioned us, in just a matter of weeks, substituting all basic greetings and phrases spoken within our household with their Portuguese equivalents. At the dinner table, we'd say *please* and *thank you* and *yes* and *no* in Portuguese. We'd begin the day with Portuguese *good morning* and end it with Portuguese *I love you, good night.* I could already feel the worldliness and culture oozing from our collective familial pores.

The first lesson did not go as planned. For the first half, the girls were fairly engaged, repeating loudly each prompt, Ivy doing so in spot-on pronunciation with Emilia blurting anything that was at least close in cadence. By the second half of the lesson, morale declined. The audio program was designed for adults, and a lack of singing and animation left the children bored, irritated, and confused.

"Come on, girls," I said the following day. "It's just thirty minutes. We're going to do this every day. Don't you want to be able to speak to people when we get to Brazil?"

"How come we didn't have to learn Australian when we went to Australia?" Ivy asked.

"Because they were speaking English," Emilia explained.

"They were?" Ivy scrunched her face in confusion.

"Yes, they just speak funny English in Australia. It's called an *absent*."

"*Accent*," I corrected.

Eventually I allowed them to sit and listen while I did the lesson, with a free pass from actually engaging in it. I figured even a daily dose of Portuguese to their youthful ears was better than nothing. This had two benefits. The first was that having to listen to the lesson without having to do it inspired fewer complaints. The second was that for me to have made any headway with the language, I needed my children to be silent. Trying to have them learn along with me only hindered my own learning, because while Ivy and I might chant *obrigada* when prompted to thank an imaginary acquaintance, Emilia's loud and simultaneous proclamation of *alibaba* invariably threw us off. I don't fault Emilia for this; she'll probably develop a phenomenal sense of direction.

I continued with Portuguese on my own, making this my main priority in my preparations for travel to Brazil (after the documentation to get us into the country and keep us alive was settled, of course). Mike listened to the same program at his own pace whenever he found himself driving alone. This gained each of us a small but worthy base, and we in turn taught our daughters in small, manageable doses.

I never want to be the type of person who journeys to a non-English-speaking land and then demands to be spoken to in English. Such people are usually also those who demand everyone in *America* speak English, and their inclination to have a world of one language and culture and mind is a sad one. Experiencing the world is enhanced exponentially when I do so with a willingness to give something of myself, rather than an expectation of what I feel I'm due. Because of that, an attempt at language learning is invaluable, and in all of my preparations for how we'd spend our time in Brazil, the most important by far was learning how to say *obrigada*.

* * *

Making Plans (Without Overdoing It)

A good plan executed today is better than a perfect plan executed at some indefinite point in the future.

—General George Patton Jr.

"Holy crap," I said as we stared at a map of Brazil in a guidebook. "This country's huge."

"No kidding," Mike agreed.

Looking at the map, we located the city from where we'd base our explorations. This wasn't a city we'd chosen because it was somewhere we'd always dreamed of going, and we've long since abandoned the pretense of having much choice in the matter. We don't choose the location; the location chooses us, in that when it comes down to it, we'll travel anywhere we have a free place to stay. In Brazil, we'd negotiated a two-month home and car exchange with a family much like our own.

"Where else in Brazil do you think we'll end up going?" Mike asked.

Brazil is the world's fifth largest country, both in terms of size and population. It occupies almost half of South America. Studying the map of the country overwhelmed us with possibilities. Because of the country's expansive geography, it hosts a variety of environments, from rain forests to deserts to savannas. We were enchanted by the wealth of potential destinations, some familiar, most not.

"The Amazon's up here," Mike said.

"We can't go all the way to Brazil and not see the Amazon."

"Agreed. I'm going to look through the guidebook and see what else sounds interesting."

"Okay," I said. "I'll leave you to it. But just make sure at some point we see a sloth."

He looked at me with a tiny bit of poorly masked disappointment and a much larger dose of tolerance.

"A sloth?"

"Yes," I confirmed. "And if I could, you know, cuddle with it, that's even better."

At heart, I am not in favor of humans interfering with wildlife. But this conviction wavers substantially when any sort of cute factor is involved. This gets complicated further by the fact that I find any nonthreatening animal cute. It doesn't have to be cute by society's high standards, just by my extremely low ones. In Australia, it had been the teddy-bear-like wombat for which I'd longed, though the wombat should be considered cute by any standards. I'd hesitate to trust anyone who doesn't see how cute wombats are.

"Visit Amazon. Cuddle with sloth. Got it," Mike said.

"But I don't think we should try to cuddle with a jaguar," Emilia added thoughtfully.

"Daddy?" Ivy said.

"Yes?"

"Just make sure they have snacks in Brazil."

* * *

Vagabonding, as a mind-set with which to approach moving through the world, does not necessitate, and in fact eschews, excessive planning. All that is required at the outset is the initial decision to go. The intent, for our family of four, is to set out with a rough framework of the trip in mind but without a set list of must-see attractions or reservations for every night. This is difficult for me. I'm a born planner, an aficionado of lists and timelines. I can logically acknowledge that when we figure things out along the way, everything works out just fine. That does not, however, mean that I can erase from my memory running through the streets of a small town in Connemara, from one hotel to the next, only to find that each had booked their last room moments before our arrival.

We'd traveled by train from Dublin, where we stayed in a hotel in the city's popular Temple Bar area. We'd booked a room for three nights in Temple Bar, but after two decided that we'd overbooked and were ready to move on. Determined not to overplan again, we simply hopped on the train headed west. We soon found that we were traveling with dozens of passengers who had hotel reservations at our destination, since our arrival coincided with the commencement of a large festival. We marveled over the beauty of Connemara's landscape of velvet green hillsides, until we considered having to spend the night sleeping on one. Whenever I remind Mike of this instance as an example of why we should plan more, he reminds me that we did, in fact, find a hotel room and no one had to sleep on a hillside under the Irish night sky. He's right, of course, but I'm a fan of avoiding such frantic moments whenever possible.

The happy medium between booking too much, as we did in Dublin, and entering a situation blind, as we did in

Connemara, is to apprise oneself of the activity in the area. If we'd known of the Connemara festival, we might have booked a room.

In addition to festivals and holiday celebrations, the travel season itself often dictates how much planning is necessary. We headed to Australia with our first month scheduled, in that we had a home in which to stay, courtesy of a home exchange. Our second month was up in the air, and we considered spending that time traveling the east coast of Australia in a camper van (caravan) before heading down to Tasmania. When we arrived in Australia and began inquiring about caravan rentals, we found ourselves playing the telephone equivalent of making a mad sprint from one booked hotel to the next. It seemed our hopes were dashed until, after dozens of phone calls, we found a rental agency with one remaining caravan. It was a near miss, as it turned out we were not the only people on the planet with the idea of traveling via caravan during Australia's peak season.

Because securing the vehicle had been such an ordeal, we proceeded to make reservations at every caravan park along our intended route for the two weeks of our travel. We'd been scared into overplanning and soon found that, with the exception of the wildly popular Byron Bay during schoolies week (also known as drunk teenagers celebrating graduation), every park we stayed at had more vacancies than occupants, and we would have been fine to travel and choose our stops along the way.

Traveling with children intensifies my inclinations to plan, especially if we're arriving late at night in an unfamiliar city. I fear the children will panic or be on the verge of a fatigue meltdown and convince myself that a hotel reservation is somehow the answer. In reality, I am the only member of my family of four who panics during such situations, as Emilia and Ivy will marvel at the city's night skyline while Mike calmly formulates a plan. Vagabonding with kids and with the right balance of planning versus spontaneity is like yoga: the more you do it, the more comfortable you'll find yourself, but nonetheless it's a lifelong practice.

Cultural research is one of my favorite activities in advance of a trip, but this should also be done in moderation. Reading too much about the generalizations assigned to people can color how you view them and interfere with genuine, meaningful interaction. That doesn't mean remaining ignorant of possibilities. Traveling without apprising yourself of your destination's basic culture is arrogant at best, dangerous at its worst. For instance, it was important for us to know that while traveling throughout Brazil, we should be vigilant with our valuables and aware of the fact that pickpockets and thieves exist (as they do everywhere), but it was equally important that we not approach every Brazilian as a scoundrel ravenous for dollars. Had we done so, we might have missed out on the scores of genuinely kind and caring strangers, people who went out of their way for us, asking nothing in return, providing us with directions, advice, friendship, and—on more than one occasion—snacks.

* * *

A New Perception of Home

The more one does and sees and feels, the more one is able to do,
and the more genuine may be one's appreciation of fundamental things
like home, and love, and understanding companionship.

—Amelia Earhart

When we first learned about home exchanges, we knew we'd found a way to alleviate the financial impact of an extended stay abroad. Hotel rooms work for a night or two but are expensive over time, a problem compounded by the constant need to eat out. Renting a house was pricey, too. But if we could simply swap homes with someone, problem solved. What could go wrong?

It turns out that completing a home exchange isn't always a simple matter, but I have no disaster story in answer to the above question, as one might expect. Nothing has ever gone wrong to the extent that the home exchange was not worth it, so we have never exchanged homes and later regretted doing so.

I initially approached the exchange concept with much of the trepidation that most first-timers feel. The idea of having other people in your space or using your stuff can provoke immediate discomfort. Walking through a series of worst-case scenarios quells these fears. What is the worst that can happen? Someone will break something or steal something? Valuables are easily relocated (personally, I find it easier simply not to own any), and a quick call to your insurance agent will switch your homeowner's insurance policy to rental coverage in the event of damage. Eventually, you learn to view your stuff as just *stuff*. The value you find in experiencing the world far outweighs what your possessions would go for at auction.

Once you get past the initial hang-ups, traveling with a home-exchange agreement in place is an ideal scenario. When you exchange your home, as opposed to simply renting it out, people take more care with their temporary surroundings, because they're hoping *you* are doing the same in *their* home. Home exchanges work wonderfully for families who have children of similar ages. We have twice exchanged with families who have two children the same ages as our own. This means that our children arrive to find "new" toys, as do the children who arrive in our house. Both homes are already equipped with children's beds, dishware, and even clothing. We've left our children's snowsuits for exchange partners, while they've left their children's sunhats and swim shirts for ours.

As the above clothing example illustrates, we like to travel in winter. As much as we love Idaho, we're not skiers or snowboarders, and my Alaskan-born-and-raised husband figures he paid all of his dues to Old Man Winter during the first eighteen years of his life. So when the weather begins to turn, we seek sunshine elsewhere. The problem with this is finding a family who *does* want to spend their winter in Idaho. Occasionally we do, as with the Brazilian family who welcomed the winter experience. But in other instances, we've had to get more creative, engaging in triangle exchanges or even taking it so far as a foursome.

Case in point: We have friends with a home in France. They agreed to a nonsimultaneous exchange with a woman in Australia. Ms. Down Under spent a month at our friends' home in France, but when our friends started planning their trip to Australia, there was a hitch. They don't have any children, but they do have a dog upon which they dote more than I do with my own children. Their dog is the center of their world. Traveling without their dog was unthinkable. And when they agreed to an exchange with Ms. Down Under, they didn't take into account that Australia's quarantine laws would force them to leave their baby at home. For them, Australia was a no-go. But now there was a dangling debt, because Ms. Down Under had already completed her stay in France. The Dog Lovers, with Ms. Down Under's permission, gave us their month's worth of time on the Sunshine Coast. In exchange, the Dog Lovers want a month's worth of time at my in-laws' home in Mexico. My in-laws agreed to this because they frequently stay with us in Idaho and because they wanted to stay with us during our trip to Brazil.

The point of all this is that circumstances need not automatically restrict travel. With creativity, patience, and an open mind, you often find that the other side of the world is closer than you think. The difficulty in completing a home exchange is not in finding exchange partners (we've used HomeExchange.com and good old word-of-mouth) or agreeing on dates, even in a complicated exchange involving three or four players. All of that works itself out. The true labor is in preparing your home.

"I think our home is basically ready," I said to Mike as we prepared for a short-term exchange with a family in Bend, Oregon.

"Yeah," Mike agreed. "I just need to fix the light that's out downstairs."

"I need to finish the paint in the hallway."

"We should move all that junk from the side of the house."

"The shower leaks."

"The bathroom fan is broken."

"A burner on the stove is out."

"Maybe we should write this down," Mike suggested.

Suddenly we'd created a daunting list of tasks for ourselves. For some reason, we are slow to make repairs and improvements for our own benefit but have no problem addressing them for strangers. This is a good thing, as by the time we are ready to depart, our house has never looked better.

Aside from repairs and upgrades, you also have to take into consideration your personal belongings. This includes paperwork like checkbooks, bills, taxes, and other important documents. Some people go so far as to keep a locked closet within their home. I settle for a safety-deposit box at the bank and a banker's box of files dropped off in the care of trusted neighbors. You also have to free up (some, not all) closet room and put away anything you wouldn't want strangers to see. For others, this probably involves exciting objects like sex toys and pot pipes. For me, this includes tucking my Spanx far from view and removing my nail fungus medication from the medicine cabinet.

* * *

The concept of *home* has become a pliable one, and the meaning of home can change and evolve at different times in life. During the spring and fall, home exists for us in the traditional sense: a structure we've known for years with living spaces to suit us. And I love this place. But I also love what home becomes at other times. For a few weeks, home was the leaky caravan in which we lived while traveling from Brisbane to Melbourne.

When we first contemplated life in a caravan, I pictured a souped-up van or a Volkswagen bus, but we opted for a camper with a toilet, in hindsight a rookie move when one considers the frequency of clean public facilities in Australia weighed against the distasteful task of regularly emptying the toilet tank of the human waste produced by a family of four. (In any case, it turned out that there weren't any smaller vehicles available.) The addition of facilities meant that our vehicle would be far greater than the size equivalent of a van. We were now firmly in RV territory. Our monstrous motor home was more than twenty-three feet long and ten feet high, which seemed enormous to me for a vehicle. In terms of a home, however, it was miniscule. We shared our bed with suitcases and books, the vehicle's cab doubled as a table, and a sink, shower, and toilet all miraculously occupied the same cubbyhole. It was cramped but tolerable, save for a few rainy days that confined us inside and made me thankful that I genuinely like my family. If we didn't get along as well as we do, that confinement could have been an epic nightmare.

Life in a camper is an excellent exercise in downsizing. You realize the folly of owning too many items, from shoes to clothes to beauty products. You begin to understand that an excess of possessions is a hindrance, and you wonder why you ever wanted them. Being stylish with a diverse wardrobe is ridiculous. Or maybe that's how I justify looking like a slob when I travel. I've become enamored with simplicity and can now recognize some of my previous packing faux pas. For instance, both Mike and I often wear baseball hats. We've taken trips before and packed five hats. Were we concerned that three might be lost at some point? Did we forget that one head requires only one hat at any given time? Whatever the reason for our lack of logic, once I recognized it, I saw it everywhere. I was carting a ridiculous excess of stuff around the world with me. More hats than I could wear, more books than I could read, outfits that don't fit, and makeup I can't be bothered to apply. Getting rid of the excess is freeing, so much so that I try to apply the same practice of simplicity to our permanent home in Idaho. Not only does this make home a more enjoyable environment, but reducing clutter also leaves us with less work when it is again time to ready our home for another family.

When you first think of various manifestations of home, you come up with houses, apartments, and hotel rooms. These are limiting, and there's great value in opening yourself up to further possibilities. In addition to caravans, we've slept in trains, ferry boats, and hostels. Like hotels, hostels vary in amenities and levels of comfort, so preconceived notions of what a hostel may be will not serve you. It's also beneficial to remain open to hotels above and below your target price range. If you were hoping for a mid-range hotel, don't turn your nose up at a downright crappy one, if that's all that's available. If you were hoping for the crappy hotel, but all you can find is one that costs more than you'd hoped to spend, this too is not the worst outcome. You can't predict every expense along the way, and there will be unexpected opportunities to recoup these funds later. Whenever I feel frustration that my accommodations are not what I anticipated, I remind myself that I'm not on vacation. I'm not in need of a killer view, fluffy robe, and room service. There have been many nights when a bed, roof, and running water do just fine, and a few others when we've had to settle for a bed and a roof. At the end of a particularly arduous journey, we might treat ourselves to above-average accommodations, but usually it's vagabonding, not vacation.

* * *

Returning after a home exchange has always been a pleasant experience. Exchange partners, without fail, have taken care to make sure that we return to our home in the condition we left it, just as we do with their home. Coming back after *renting* out our house is a different story. We rented out our home for the latter half of our Australia trip, grateful that we'd have some cash to put toward the plane tickets and to make up for the fact that, compared to other travels and for a variety of reasons, it was an expensive trip.

We traveled for twenty-four hours to find our home in a disastrous state. Everything—floors, counters, and doors—felt sticky.

"What happened to the cleaning company?" Mike asked.

"I don't know."

We put our bags down and commanded the girls to sit on the couch and watch television, to which they gleefully agreed.

"You better give them a call," Mike said. "I don't even feel like we should unpack until we deal with this."

"Are you sure they came and cleaned?" I demanded on the phone, speaking to the company's owner.

"She was there all day," he assured me, referring to the cleaner. "I came to help out myself. It looked like someone had been sick downstairs, and we spent most of the time trying to deal with that. Honestly, we did the best we could." The owner and the cleaner had used all of the available time between the renters' departure and our return to try to put the house right again. I was glad I hadn't seen it in its worst state.

I thanked him for their efforts, and Mike and I set about the task of cleaning the house from top to bottom. Mike doesn't share my obsessive cleaning compulsions, so the fact that he was disturbed by the state of things let me know that it wasn't just me. The twenty-four hours of travel had drained us, but we knew that there would be no rest until we'd mopped the floors, scrubbed the bathrooms, and located a host of unfortunate items to be discarded, like frozen breast milk and half-eaten, petrified cheese sticks.

You might think that the state of the home was because we'd rented it to irresponsible youth, or a bachelor or bachelorette party, but as the breast milk and cheese sticks indicate, that wasn't the case. We'd rented the home to a nice Mormon family who were in town to celebrate a relative's return from his mission. I'd mistakenly assumed these nondrinking, pious people of exceptional family values would be great tenants, but in hindsight, I might have preferred to rent to a gaggle of drunken twenty-one-year-olds. At least they might have left vodka in the freezer as opposed to breast milk.

When the home was clean and we permitted the girls to roam freely, they wandered into their room.

"I remember these toys!" Ivy exclaimed.

"Ooh, look, my bed!" Emilia said.

"Mommy, I like this home," Ivy added. "I'm glad we came back to this one."

It took the innocence of these statements to remind me that, while the renters had been disappointing, the trip was worth it. No matter the state of our home upon our return, no matter if an hour or two of cleaning is required to right what's been left askew, the trip is always worth it. And sometimes we have to recognize that it's our home, whether rented or exchanged, that helps make the trip a reality.

* * *

But Think of the Children!

In school, you're taught a lesson and then given a test.
In life, you're given a test that teaches you a lesson.

—Tom Bodett

"So, I guess we'll have to travel in the summers then, when the kids are out of school," I said. This was before our first extended trip with children, when Mike was slowly working to change my thinking, because I still didn't get it.

"Why do you think it's important that the kids stay in school?" he asked.

I was speechless. *Why* did I think it was important? Why were we even having this conversation? You couldn't take your kids out of school in the middle of the school year. It just wasn't done. They'd fall behind, lose friends, be ostracized and alone.

"Well, aside from the obvious of missing out on their education," I said, "what are we supposed to do with them?" I had to give voice to the fact that while every cell of my body is charged with love for my kids, I also prize the hours in which they are at school or daycare. If they weren't in school or daycare, they would be with me. All the time. If there's one thing I've learned about myself as a parent in the last eight years, it's that I am atrocious in the role of stay-at-home mom. I have great respect for those who succeed in this role without self-medicating through it. I am not one of those mothers.

"There are schools all over the world," Mike said. "There are online programs."

Sure, there are schools all over the world, but would we really send our children there? I had this thought for only a moment before recognizing the xenophobia of it. Of course there would be excellent schools and childcare facilities the world over. Just as there would be mediocre ones. There was no reason to think that schools and daycares in America were somehow superior to foreign ones. I remembered my early hunt for a daycare in Boise and the dozen facilities I left, thinking, *There's no way in hell I'm leaving my kid there*, before finally finding a clear winner.

"But what will their school here say when we tell them we're leaving for three months?"

Would the community shun us? Report us to Child Protective Services? Would school administrators brand me as a BM? (That's Bad Mom, not bowel movement, though they are viewed in similar light.) The teachers would hate me for disrupting the school year. Would they even let us back in the class upon our return?

"Amanda, who *cares* what they say?"

Of course, *I* cared. I was the rule-following product of a scheduled and regimented society. You went to school, got a job, worked, and died. That was the formula for a happy American life. If we deviated from that, would that make us deviants?

"Amanda," he said my name a second time, a cue that what was coming was important, and important to him that I understand. "Don't you think that our kids are going to learn more from three months in another country than they will from three months in a kindergarten classroom?"

That was my moment of understanding, when I stopped worrying about following convention and gave serious consideration to what it would mean in terms of impact on our children. What would our children truly gain? Traveling wasn't a hardship on them to appease our selfish desire to live abroad. Traveling would be *good* for them and provide an education that couldn't be quantified.

Once I recognized that education and travel are nearly interchangeable, I steeled myself to any admonitions that would come my way for not giving my children an uninterrupted school year. But they never came. Other people saw the value of the experience for the kids long before I did.

I still feared the teachers. Surely they would disagree.

"I'm really nervous about this," I confided to Mike on our way to Emilia's elementary school.

"About what?"

"About this. About this conference."

"You're nervous about a parent-teacher conference for our kindergartner? Maybe you need to consider Xanax or Valium or one of those other calm-you-down drugs."

"It's not the parent-teacher conference part. It's the by-the-way-we're-pulling-our-kid-out-of-school-for-three-months part."

"I thought we got over this conversation—didn't we?"

"We got over it in terms of me agreeing that we're not going to let a traditional public school education hold us back, but that doesn't mean I've surmounted my fear of how Mr. Li will react."

Mr. Li taught Emilia during her half day of immersion in Mandarin Chinese. I'd volunteered in the class enough to develop rapport with him. He was a nice man. He was great with kids. But I was already someone who feared confrontation and reprimand. The idea of experiencing confrontation and reprimand in *Mandarin* was downright terrifying. It was an intriguing language but also one that, when spoken by Mr. Li, sounded fairly harsh. And that was just when he was counting from one to ten.

"Well, *I'm* not worried," Mike said. "After all, we're the parents."

I figured that Mike's admission of ease meant that he'd take the lead when delivering the news. As I sat across the table from Mr. Li, in a tiny plastic chair, which I felt might crumble under the weight of my ass at any moment, Mr. Li let us know of Emilia's progress and impeccable handwriting. "The only problem Emilia has is that she gets very upset if she doesn't draw it perfectly. She has better Chinese handwriting than Chinese kids, but she's easily frustrated." We nodded, letting him know that we were well aware of Emilia's ability to melt down in the pursuit of unattainable perfection. "Other than that, she's doing great," he assured us. "Do you have any questions or concerns?" he asked. I elbowed Mike, who remained silent by my side.

"Well, yes," I finally conceded, if for no other reason than to fill the silence. "Actually there is something I wanted to talk about." I offered nothing further.

"Okay," Mr. Li encouraged. "Go ahead." He looked concerned. I wondered what he might be anticipating. What were the usual topics parents struggled to discuss during conferences? Did he anticipate news of a soon-to-be broken home or that Emilia would soon begin the process of gender transitioning?

"We're leaving the country!" I blurted.

Mr. Li's face registered shock. I'd delivered the news in an alarming manner, one that implied our impending travel was due to the witness protection program or life on the lam.

"We'll be living in Mexico for three months," Mike interjected. "So we wanted to know if you have any materials you could provide us before we go, so that we might keep up with the schoolwork taking place in the classroom."

"Oh." Mr. Li smiled with relief. "Of course!" He looked at me again, and concern replaced his momentary relief. Maybe Xanax wasn't a bad idea.

In the years since that first trip, every one of our girls' teachers, when learning of our travels and interruption to their instruction and curriculum, has responded with, "That's fantastic. What can I do to help?"

My daughters' education is now a hybrid system of schooling that explores more than the options of public school versus homeschooling, because just as I had to change my thinking on the value of travel versus a complete school year in the public school system, I then had to educate myself on the variety of ways to educate my children. Removing my kids from school didn't necessarily mean I had to homeschool them.

During that three-month trip to Mexico, when Ivy was three and Emilia was five, they attended a Montessori school. Five days a week, we would drive them a mile down a dirt road, make a left at the big cactus, and drop them off at a bilingual Montessori for both local Mexican children and expats. There were certain things to get used to, like needing to remind our children to watch for rattlesnakes on the playground, but other aspects of the school were less scary and more endearing. A yellow brick road led through the school garden, decorated along the way with *Wizard of Oz* characters, and the schoolhouse cat watched over the children, only biting them on occasion. Getting bitten in the course of a school day is unfortunate, but better cat than rattlesnake.

At the end of each school day, Emilia and I continued her studies so we might keep up with the Mandarin curriculum provided by Mr. Li. While I have many skills, Mandarin is not one of them, but I did my best to guide her in tracing the characters and reciting numbers. When she moved to first grade, we abandoned the Mandarin school in favor of the public school two blocks from our home, so any failures I had in keeping up with Emilia's Chinese instruction became moot anyway.

My panic at giving my kindergartner a geographically and linguistically diverse introduction to school was not shared by my five-year-old and stemmed only from convention. Nothing about learning Chinese or attending a bilingual school in Mexico was intimidating to Emilia. It was only intimidating to me. And when I realized that telling her "you're going to learn Chinese" was the same to her ears as "you're going to learn to tell time," I was able to let go of my own fears, which I'd been unknowingly projecting on her.

As chaotic as that year of education seemed, from language immersion in the United States to Mexican Montessori then back to Mandarin, it turned out to be one of the most orderly years she's had. Now, school has evolved into an even more diverse and unregulated affair. In the States, Emilia and Ivy are typical American children in the public school system. When we travel, we engage in a hybrid of homeschooling, online programs, and materials provided by their teachers back home. Both children keep journals, an entry of which might be a drawing, chronicle of the day's events, or hopes for the future (I hope one day I will find a baby rainbow unicorn). Technology enables us to supplement the materials we have with math programs disguised as games, like Prodigy.com. Full-time vagabonding families can enroll their children in free, accredited online schools like Connections Academy or K12, something we may explore in time.

The element of travel adds the educational enhancement of learning about and experiencing the culture in which we find ourselves. An assignment might be to learn about the origins of a country's flag and draw it, or to ask a local about the three biggest challenges facing the person's region, or to list ten similarities and ten differences between the flora and fauna of our host country and America.

I always assume the flag assignment will be a hit, because aside from learning about the origin of a flag and the meaning behind its elements, it's basically coloring. Both Australia and Brazil have, to my mind, visually interesting flags, more than three bands of color, to which so many countries seem to default. You have the opportunity to develop a symbol to represent an entire nation, and all you can come up with is three stripes? Lame. Even worse: the number of countries that have chosen this pattern in the overused red, white, and blue combo. I'm looking at you, France, Luxembourg, Netherlands, and Russia.

As we began a few hours of homeschooling in Brazil, I had the bright idea of the flag assignment. What I'd forgotten, from attempting the same assignment the year before in Australia, is that visually interesting flags reduce my children to tears.

"I can't do it, Mom! I can't draw a circle," Emilia moaned.

"What do you mean you can't draw a circle? Of course you can draw a circle."

"But it won't be perfect!" she cried.

"It doesn't have to be perfect," I insisted, but her face flushed, and her eyes welled. In such instances, I waver between frustration with my daughter, flashbacks of the parent-teacher conference with Mr. Li, and the knowledge that I am the parent who passed this impossible curse on to my child. I'm not sure when I finally outgrew the quest for perfection myself, but now the concept is a laughable one.

"Why don't we find a circle we can trace?" I suggested. This began a thirty-minute assessment of various jars, cups, and vases until we located the perfect diameter. Both Ivy and Emilia traced a perfect circle. I used a ruler to outline the diamond around the circle and eventually found myself sketching the flag in pencil for both of them. They could do the coloring and final touches, and perhaps we'd avoid further tantrums. This is a perfect illustration of the fact that I'm not skilled when it comes to teaching. I cave too easily to whining, because I can't stand the thought of it leading to more whining, and I end up doing the work for them, when they'd be better served if I presented them with the task and remained hands-off until its completion.

"There are too many *stars!*" Ivy moaned. "I'm not *good* at stars!" And that was when I remembered flag-homeschool day in Australia, which had passed with similar amounts of whining and tears. The Australian flag, like its Brazilian counterpart, has many stars. Unless you are an artist, or perhaps astronomer, stars are difficult to draw, no matter what your age. I hastily drew an abundance of crappy stars on each of their flags and told them I didn't want to hear another word about it.

"Let's write in the words," I said, mustering false cheer. *"Ordem e Progresso.* What do you think that means?"

"How should we know, Mom? We don't *speak* Portuguese," Emilia informed me, and I wished for a principal to which I could send both my children.

"It means Order and Progress." By that point in the trip, we'd spent enough time in Brazil to gain a deep appreciation for the country and to know, without a doubt, that order and progress were not its strengths.

The cultural assignments involving interviews with locals about their culture, economy, and ecology are more successful. My children behave far better in the company of people other than their parents. These assignments also allow us to take our children's education beyond sitting at a table with pencil and paper, which has become extremely important in light of the fact that when we travel, they don't have daily recess in which to play with friends on a playground. The basic interaction with people is as valuable (if not more) as the knowledge they gain by asking questions.

Both girls miss their classmates and friends at home, but they're able to accept that separation as a temporary sacrifice. They understand that there is equal value in interacting with people of different cultures.

"I miss Jasper," Ivy confided in me after six weeks abroad.

"I miss Jasper, too," I said. I refrained from voicing that I also missed drinking wine with Jasper's mom while the two girls played dress-up.

"And when we go back, maybe we can go to Jasper's house and play dress-up," she said.

"Absolutely," I agreed. *And drink wine.*

"I want to give a really cool gift to Jasper when we go back. A cool Brazil gift. Will you make sure you put that on the list?"

"Cool Brazil gift for Jasper. Got it."

* * *

Part of vagabonding has been gaining the understanding that there is never one correct way to do things, and our children's education is no exception. What may work for us one year may not be the best system for the following year. As someone innately drawn to the idea of formulating a plan and sticking to it, it hasn't been easy for me to periodically evaluate our education plan and change our approach as needed. Just as children pass through grades and curriculums, they also outgrow learning methods. Somehow, by drawing on a variety of materials and applications, we seem to manage each trip by finding a hybrid system that works for us. Our approach may be unconventional and difficult at times, but with patience, care, and perhaps a large sheet of star-shaped stickers, we'll do just fine.

* * *

What Do You Really Need to Take with You?

I hate pain, despite my ability to tolerate it beyond all known parameters, which is not necessarily a good thing.

—Hunter S. Thompson

"**M**om, I want to pack my own bag this time," Emilia said. "I know how to do it."

"Are you sure? I'm happy to do it for you. In fact, don't worry about it at all, and I'll pack while you two are at school."

"Ooh! I want to pack my bag, too," Ivy said.

"I'll tell you what. Why don't you girls each make a pile of what you want to bring and then tell me when you're done?"

"Okay," Emilia agreed. "But don't look. You're not allowed to see until we're finished."

Whenever my children tell me not to look, I begin mentally preparing myself for the chaos I will face when the ban is lifted. Fifteen minutes later, the call came.

"Mom, we're ready!" Ivy yelled.

I entered their bedroom to find them each standing proudly next to a pile of their respective belongings.

"Great job, girls." This was the required statement of encouragement before tearing their work apart. "Ivy, that's a lot of stuffed animals."

"Yes, I'm bringing Sparkle and Baby Snow Leopard and Pablo and Twinkle and Pinkie Pie."

"That's too many, Ivy," Emilia instructed. I thought she might do my job for me, but then she added, "You should only bring three."

"Hmm." Ivy tapped a finger to her chin. "That's going to be tough, but I think I'll go with Sparkle, Baby Snow Leopard, and Pinkie Pie."

"Actually, Ivy," I interjected, "I don't think we're going to bring *any* stuffed animals on this trip."

Her mouth dropped open, and she stared at me in disbelief, as if I'd told her we'd be traveling nude.

"You can still bring blankie, but I think it's better if we leave the stuffed animals here."

"Not even Sparkle?"

"Sparkle will be much safer if we leave her here."

I wondered if tears or tantrum would follow, but she muttered a sullen assent.

"How about me?" Emilia stood proud with her hands on her hips, sure that she had avoided any such mistakes.

"That's an awful lot of books." Two dozen paperbacks formed a single, precarious tower.

"Well, reading is good for my brain. And I don't think they're going to have movies or toys in the jungle, so . . ."

"All valid points," I agreed. "But we have to remember that we're going to carry everything we bring, from city to jungle to city. So how about we bring one book for the jungle—"

"*One* book?"

"And the rest of the time you can read e-books."

"Whoa, that was a close one. For a second there, I thought you were telling me that I could only read one book on the whole trip."

Her panic delighted me; she viewed books as important as food.

Not all of the possessions they selected needed reassessing. They had essentials like flashlights and underwear but also an inordinate amount of long sleeves in light of the fact that we were headed for a tropical climate.

While it's easy to dismiss their packing errors as the faux pas of children, I'm guilty of making similar mistakes on an adult scale. Women in particular struggle with packing light when it comes to toiletries. As American female consumers, we've somehow bought into the bullshit of an industry that sells millions of products to change the way we look. For my hair alone, I've packed hair dryers, flat irons, hair spray, and multiple styling products, when all I really need is a brush. This is especially ridiculous in light of the fact that, though nearing midlife, I have yet to learn how to successfully style my own hair.

For the rest of the body, there are scores of other products designed to lengthen, lessen, tighten, conceal, lift, tuck, or enhance, depending on which body part needs my focus. It's only when I'm packing for a trip that I realize what a scam this industry is and I see these unnecessary accoutrements as very sparkly shackles. I'm trying to get better, to shed those shackles, but it's hard.

Medicines should merit more consideration than vanity items. We try to travel with limited quantities of children's Tylenol, antacids, cold medicines, ibuprofen, Imodium, and a prescription for something to combat traveler's diarrhea. The reason we travel with *limited* quantities of these import- ant little drugs is that the world is chock-full of well-stocked pharmacies with incredibly helpful pharmacists who are not above engaging in charades to figure out your ailment when there's a language barrier. If we travel with plenty of cold medicine but no Imodium, no one will get a cold and someone will be desperate for Imodium. I'm seasoned enough to *never* travel without Imodium. Rarely can we predict the nature of a body's impending sickness, so we find it best to travel with just enough to get us by until we can reach one of the afore- mentioned pharmacies. They are never far, on street corners and in grocery stores, airports, and shopping malls around the globe.

The first time you pack for a two- or three-month trip, the inclination is to pack two or three months' worth of clothing. You'd be better suited to pack the same amount of clothes you would if only traveling for a week, because if you're on the road for more than a week, chances are you'll end up search- ing for a washing machine or begin washing your clothes in a sink. There's no need to plan your clothing for every day of the trip. I *know* this. I am a rational and logical being, but it is near impossible to implement. There have been times when I've almost succeeded, when I've carefully selected the contents of my luggage, each item of which is chosen based on its limited size, weight, and the fact that it is indispens- able to the success of the trip. At the last minute, however, just before I leave home and lock the door behind me, I am compelled to grab handfuls of clothing that I *might* need. Nine times out of ten, *might* means *won't*. Overcoming the urge to muddy the suitcase with extraneous and unnecessary items is like corking a bottle of wine instead of polishing it off. I know there are people who can actually do such a thing, but to date, I am not one of them.

You cannot pack light by reading a guide on how to do so, or by downloading a checklist from the Internet, because these methods imply that someone else could pack for you. But someone else might require solution for contact lenses or tampons or an inhaler, items that would have no use for a traveler like my husband. When it comes to what we need to feel comfortable moving about in the world, we each have a highly individualized list.

The difficulties of efficient packing compound further with children. Consider blankies, sippy cups, strollers, diapers, car seats, and beloved but worn-to-the-point-of-disgusting stuffed animals (which Ivy has thankfully agreed to "keep safe" at home from this point forward). Life gets a little easier once you shed the strollers and diaper bags. But the compulsion remains to bring more than you need, because that's how we react to going into the unknown. We try to prepare, guessing at possible calamities, but preparing for the unknown is never fully possible. If we took only what we needed, we'd travel with food, water, and shelter, all of which are frowned upon by airlines.

When it comes down to it, you need far less than you think. No matter how many times I think I've made headway in efficient packing (for my hair, I've finally confined myself to a brush and one styling product, the latter of which I never use), each trip sheds new light on areas for improvement. I have yet to travel to a tropical location without carting along a gallon-sized Ziploc full of sunscreen. Brazil was no exception. If we'd flown directly into the Amazon jungle, the sunscreen might have made sense, but we stayed in a variety of cities before traveling to the jungle. The cities boasted pharmacies on every corner, as plentiful as the ubiquitous Walgreens and Rite-Aids in the United States. Each of these Brazilian pharmacies offered dozens of options of sunscreen, and each bottle of sunscreen cost about a fifth of what we'd paid for an equivalent product from the States. The same could be said of shampoo, soap, toothpaste, and first aid products. Not to say that I plan on traveling without these necessities in the future, but I hope to learn to travel with just enough to get us through the first few days of a trip.

* * *

"Mom," Emilia said. "It hurts when I lift my shoulders."

We were midway through our Brazilian adventure in Itacaré, a small tourist town in Bahia's cocoa zone, south of Salvador.

"Your muscles are just sore from all that exercise," I said. She'd spent a good part of the morning playing in the surf. "It's good for you."

"I don't think it's my muscles."

I turned to my daughter and realized, with an immediate wave of horror and disappointment in myself, that I'd lapsed in the sunscreen applications and Emilia suffered a terrible sunburn as a result.

"Ooh, that's not good," Mike said.

"We're horrible parents."

"No, we're not. Are we out of sunscreen?"

I held up the gallon-sized bag of sunscreen, which seemed never to diminish, no matter how much we used.

"You're right," he corrected himself. "We're horrible parents."

We slathered her shoulders in aloe, which did little to ease her pain or our conscience, and spent the following week assuring her that despite the patchy appearance of her peeling skin, all would be back to normal by the time she returned to her American classroom.

* * *

When Emilia was eight weeks old, and I was grappling with the fact that a baby requires ten times her body weight in additional gear, we found ourselves on a small island in Sitka, Alaska. Sitka is a city primarily located on the west side of Baranof Island in Alaska's Alexander Archipelago. The city includes other islands, like Kruzof, home to the dormant Mount Edgecumbe volcano, and countless specks in the sea dotting the Sitka Sound. Traveling through the Eastern Channel, you pass Breast Island and the Ball Islets, none of which resemble anatomy on a map. We stayed on nearby Bamdoroshni Island where five families had built homes in the early seventies.

My in-laws were house-sitting in one of them, and we'd come to crash the party. The house had a gorgeous view, as any secluded home on a tiny island will, but the home also suffered from moderate disrepair and neglect. All homes need maintenance over time, and I'm convinced that dealing with repairs is more difficult when living in any sort of remote location (especially when one must travel by boat to reach a store). For a small repair at our home in Idaho, Mike is apt to make half a dozen trips to the hardware store. On an island in Alaska, there's no such thing as a quick trip to Home Depot.

I'm completely capable of handling states of disrepair and neglect, except for the fact that on Bamdoroshni Island, I was a first-time mom with an eight-week-old baby. Hundreds of admonitions against exposing my child to harmful elements swirled in my brain.

"You doing okay?" Mike asked, entering the upstairs bedroom allotted to us. It was a child's room, filled with adolescent belongings and posters taped haphazardly to the wall. We slept as a family of three on a worn mattress on the floor.

"I'm fine," I said. "Can you hold her?"

I handed Mike our daughter and gathered up the million pieces of a hand-me-down breast pump. "I just need to go downstairs and wash these." I had a love-hate relationship with the breast pump. On the one hand, it was extremely convenient to have a bottle of breast milk at the ready to save me from constantly having to bare my boobs. On the other hand, I never quite warmed to the idea or act of being milked.

"Okay." Mike frowned. "Just so you know, my dad went fishing."

I had no idea why he felt the need to share such information, and I proceeded downstairs with the goal of hot, soapy water and a sterile surface where my breast pump components might dry.

I entered the kitchen to find the sink brimming with salmon filets ready to be vacuum-sealed and frozen.

"Check it out!" My father-in-law beamed, motioning to his catch.

"Wow," I said, trying to muster the enthusiasm he craved. "That's great."

"Yeah," he boomed. "Not a bad haul."

I looked around for a clean counter on which to set the items I needed to wash, but it seemed everything was covered in errant fish scales. I breathed, told myself to go with the flow, and retreated upstairs.

The following day, an excruciating case of mastitis greeted me. Mastitis is a common infection among breastfeeding mothers. It is incredibly painful when full blown, as evidenced by the angry red lightning bolts streaking across my chest. At the time, I didn't know what plagued me, why I had it, or what the remedy was.

Mike and his mom had boated (past Breast Island) into town for a few errands when I discovered the mastitis via sudden excruciating pain and the aforementioned lightning bolts. So I found myself stranded on an island in Alaska with a breast ailment and no one to turn to but my father-in-law. The situation was less than ideal.

I fed Emilia with a bottle made from formula, which I used to supplement breast milk, because attempting to breast-feed her brought me to tears. After draining the bottle, she belched and drifted into the contented sleep of a well-fed baby. I placed her in her car seat, grabbed my phone, and held it above my head in hopes of finding a signal. This was before laptops, ever-present Internet, and smartphones. The best I could hope for was a phone call to a female friend, someone with access to information and who wouldn't mind discussing my mammary glands.

"Hello?"

"Kelly, it's Amanda! Help me! I'm stuck on an island in Alaska with my father-in-law, and there's something wrong with my boobs!"

"Oh, uh, what is it you want me to do?"

"Are you near a computer? I need to find out what's wrong with me."

My friend spent the next ten minutes diagnosing me with the help of WebMD and assured me that if I procured antibiotics, everything would be okay.

I remained in hiding until Mike and my mother-in-law returned, sure that if I showed my face, my father-in-law would instinctively deduce that I had some sort of breast ailment, which would lead to a conversation I was determined to avoid.

"Mike, I need a doctor," I said when he entered our temporary lodgings.

"Why? What's wrong? Is Emilia okay?"

I lifted my shirt.

"Yes!" he affirmed. "Let's get you to a doctor."

We took the boat into town, hopped into my in-laws' ancient Suzuki, and drove to the medical clinic. In the waiting room, it seemed we came across half a dozen of Mike's female friends from high school.

"Oh, you're Mike's wife," each would say with a smile. "It's so nice to meet you!" We'd exchange pleasantries for a moment until the inevitable, "Oh my gosh, what are you here for? Is everything okay?" At which point I would mutter under my breath, retreat to a corner, and accept the fact that I was branding myself as Mike Turner's slightly odd and rude wife.

A sympathetic female doctor (who thankfully had not attended high school with my husband) gently prodded my breasts for a minute and prescribed the necessary antibiotics. I was soon on the mend.

My distress with our accommodations (which were free, and we're all familiar with the fact that beggars lack the luxury of choice) and the scale-covered kitchen turned immaterial in the face of needing competent medical care. As angry as I was with my own boobs, for what I viewed as a completely unmerited betrayal, at least they provided some perspective on the essentials when my OCD tendencies led me astray. Modern comforts and conveniences are not necessities; modern medicine is.

* * *

When we leave a location, whether that's home at the beginning of a trip, or departing one city to head to another, there's always a momentary panic. What are we forgetting? While I used to mentally race through an endless list, including toothbrushes, ibuprofen, snacks, and doubt over whether I'd packed enough socks, I now waste no worry on these easily replaceable items. When you narrow it down to the basics, it becomes simple. As long as we are in possession of our children, passports, wallets, and phones, we're in good shape. With those few items, I know that we are not *entirely* horrible parents, we can get where we're going, pay for what we've forgotten, and call for help if needed.

* * *

Adventures in Street Food

You don't need a silver fork to eat good food.
—Paul Prudhomme

When we prepare for travel with our kids, I panic at the thought of feeding them. Fortunately, we have always been able to locate instant noodles and bananas, which my kids would happily live on. And much to Ivy's relief, snacks have proven to be a worldwide phenomenon. Everywhere we've traveled has its own version of the typical kid foods: pizza, granola bars, chips, fries, and chicken nuggets. There have been times when I've resented the availability of such foods, wishing we had to survive on plantains and piranha, so that we might shed the processed foods we're used to, expand our horizons, and feel some measure of gratitude for the plentitude of options typically afforded us.

Exploring street food is the easiest way to enjoy local fare and avoid the trap of a diet limited to the aforementioned and beloved instant noodles and bananas. After three months in any town on Mexico's Baja Peninsula, you'll learn where to find the best fish tacos and tortas and how much they cost (not much). You acclimate to plastic plates sheathed in plastic bags before food is placed on them, and you learn to order *para llevar* (to-go) if the hordes of flies are prohibitive. And when you travel as a family of four and are still recovering from the shock of purchasing four international round-trip airline tickets, the price of street food is just right.

"Mom, this quesadilla tastes different," Ivy whined.

Mike took the quesadilla from her hand and helped himself. "That's because it's *good*, Ivy. This is way better than the quesadillas we have at home. These are fresh tortillas. It's not different; it's *better*."

"It's cheese and a tortilla," I added. "Those are two of the tastiest things on the planet. How can you not like that?"

"After this, can we go out for ice cream?" she asked, ignoring my question.

"No," I answered. She had no problem with Mexican ice cream, which, while also better than what she was used to, was undeniably different. In addition to the usual suspects of chocolate, vanilla, and strawberry, we'd sampled such flavors as rosemary, salt and pepper, and sweet corn.

"Eat your quesadilla," Mike instructed. "Or would you rather have a bite of mine?" He offered his taco, a tortilla filled with steak, pico de gallo, and more jalapenos than any human should consume in one sitting.

"Um, no thanks. I think I actually do like the quesadilla."

As frustrated as I get with my daughters' picky eating habits, the exploration of food around the world has made slow but notable progress in cultivating a more diverse diet. By the end of our Mexico trip, quesadillas were not grudgingly accepted but requested. (Not that I am in any way asserting cheese and tortillas constitute a diverse diet.)

On Australia's Sunshine Coast, they were more adventurous than Mike and I when it came to sampling visually off-putting but apparently delicious cocktail sausages. In Melbourne, both girls gleefully gobbled up half a plaxte of calamari (until I made the mistake of telling them that they were eating squid).

We found that the best food in Tasmania's tiny coastal town of Triabunna came not from a restaurant but from the Fish Van, which sat near the marina and offered a variety of food but specialized in fish and chips.

"Wow, there's quite a queue," Mike said after parking near the Fish Van.

"A queue?"

"Yeah, it means there's a line."

"I know what it means," I said. "I'm just surprised to hear you say it."

"What? I'm practically a local by this point."

"Uh-huh," I said, with no effort to disguise my sarcasm.

"So, I'll just go order a few different things," he suggested.

"Sounds good," I agreed. "I'll wait here with the kids."

The girls and I watched from the car as Mike took his place at the end of the *queue*. Ten minutes later, he returned to the car with paper cones of fish and fries.

"I have no idea what that woman said to me," he said.

"What do you mean?"

"The woman working the Fish Van. I couldn't understand a word she said."

"Was she not speaking English?"

"She was, but her accent was so strong, I honestly have no idea what she said."

"What happened to *practically a local* taking your place in the *queue?*" I asked.

"Forget I ever said that."

"It smells good, Daddy," Ivy called from the backseat as Mike drove us back to our hotel.

"It sure does," I agreed. "What did you order?"

"I have no idea."

"What?"

"I didn't know what any of the types of fish were," he said, and I knew this was hard for him to admit. As a born-and-raised Alaskan, Mike prides himself on his knowledge of the sea. Not only does he harbor extensive knowledge of seafood, but he also knows what foods to order in different countries, depending on the proximity of the fish's natural habitat to whatever our location may be at the time. Though we had no idea what it was we actually consumed that evening, it was delicious, the children offered no complaint, and we went back the next night for more.

In Brazil, our children not only sampled piranha, they ate piranha for which they had themselves fished in an Amazonian tributary. Acai sorbet became a favorite treat, along with coconut water consumed directly from a large, green coconut. Which isn't to say they've transcended their love of all things fried and/or processed. With a chance to explore some of Bahia's best street food, both girls immediately identified a van with a picture of Scooby-Doo on the side as their establishment of choice. I watched as the vendor prepared a customer's hot dog, topping it off with not only ketchup but also corn, olives, and a variety of intriguing sauces. When I asked him for two hot dogs with only ketchup, he looked disappointed.

"You don't want any of this?" he asked in Portuguese.

"No," I answered. "Only ketchup. For children."

He obliged but in a bewildered state, apparently not used to someone eschewing his hot-dogs-turned-works-of-art.

"What are you going to get?" I asked Mike after the children were well into their hot dogs. Food carts offered kabobs, Greek wraps, and shrimp fritters in dough made of beans, which I was determined to try.

"I think we should go there first," Mike said. I followed his line of sight to an endless row of stalls. Instead of food offerings, these were individual bars stocked with numerous bottles of booze. Each held an enormous drink menu. Like most patrons, we ignored the menus and opted for caipirinhas, the national drink made of cachaça (alcohol distilled from sugarcane), sugar, and fresh, muddled lime.

"You guys sure do like those lime drinks," Emilia commented.

"You have ketchup on your face," I said, ignoring her observation.

"What are you guys going to eat?" Ivy asked.

"I'm going for kabobs," Mike said.

"What's kabobs?" Ivy asked.

"Meat on a stick," he answered.

"Man," said Emilia. "Brazil is just like meat-topia."

"Yes," I agreed. "They do love meat here."

Mike ordered chicken kabobs and steak kabobs, both of which Ivy sampled.

"You mean that hot dog didn't fill you up?" he asked.

"No," she said. "My meal stomach isn't full yet."

"Your meal stomach?"

"Yes. Emilia and I decided we each have two stomachs. Her meal stomach is full; mine isn't yet. Our dessert stomachs are empty."

"How about your chicken heart stomach?" he asked, offering her a bite from a gruesome kabob of speared chicken hearts.

"No, thanks," she said.

"What are you going to get, Mom?" Emilia asked.

"I really want to try the acarajé," I said, indicating the stand where the shrimp fritters were sold. I'd been told of acarajé by our guide, a young Dutch expat who assisted us for ten days of coastal exploration during our two months in Brazil. I've never shied away from seafood, and the description of the dish intrigued me. Until I sat with it in my hands. Mike and the girls stared expectantly at me, waiting for me to take a bite. I'd forgotten that in Brazil, shrimp are often consumed with the shells and tails intact. I surveyed the shrimp, nestled with sauces in the fried shell of bean dough. Consuming shrimp shells and tails seemed wrong, like eating plastic. How were such things digestible? But obviously they were, as this was a popular street food and the acarajé vendor was doing a steady business.

I silently balked for only a moment. How was I ever to expect my children to expand their culinary horizons if I turned my nose up at the food in my hands because it was *different?* I ate the acarajé, every last tail included. I didn't rush back for a second helping, but I was glad I'd tried it. It was a good reminder that if I wanted my children to be open to new foods, I owed it to them to order adventurously myself.

Occasionally I've given my children reason to be suspicious of the foods I encourage them to eat by failing to test something myself before giving it to them. This may seem like a rookie move, but it's one I make when lulled in by what appears to be the most innocuous of foods in a familiar and safe environment. When Emilia was approaching toddlerhood, I thought nothing of giving her a bite of mashed potatoes. It seemed so innocent, and rather than eating from a food truck in South America, we were dining at a previously vetted restaurant in our hometown of Boise. I thought nothing could go wrong, but after one bite, Emilia's face contorted, and a shudder shook her tiny body. She didn't cry but seemed stunned into silence.

"What did you give her?" Mike asked.

"It was just a bite of mashed potatoes," I said.

"Are they hot? Did you burn her mouth?"

"No! I couldn't have. It was just a tiny bite from the very top."

Mike looked at me with accusation and doubt. I took a bite myself.

"Oh," I said quietly.

"What is it?"

"Well, they're not just mashed potatoes."

"What do you mean?" He reached over with his fork and took a bite of what would otherwise have been perfectly normal, delicious mashed potatoes (had they not been mixed with massive amounts of wasabi).

Most of us remember our first taste of wasabi as shocking, to say the least. I'm a fan of horseradish in all forms but had not intended to inflict it on my child at such a young age.

Seven years later, we sat in a diner, just blocks from the wasabi incident. Mike and I had ordered for ourselves and Ivy, but Emilia wanted to order on her own.

"I would like the scrambled eggs, please," she said politely. "But I do not want the mashed browns. I don't like mashed browns. Instead of the mashed browns, could I get another egg added to my scrambled eggs?" I willed the waitress not to correct her.

"Of course, dear," the waitress said and headed for the kitchen.

"So, Emilia," Mike said. "You don't like mashed browns?"

"No, I do not."

"Do you like mashed potatoes?" I asked.

"No, I do not."

"Okay, Sam-I-am. Why don't you like mashed potatoes?"

"Well, I guess I like them a little bit. But I don't like them when they have stuff *on* them."

Surely she was speaking of gravy or an excess of butter (though who doesn't like gravy or an excess of butter?). There was no way she was carrying a dislike for potatoes in various forms because of the wasabi incident seven years prior. And yet, I swear that for a brief moment, she was remembering something, and her face almost imperceptibly contorted as her body shook with a tiny shudder.

* * *

Staying Safe

If you wish to travel far and fast, travel light.
Take off all your envies, jealousies, unforgiveness,
selfishness and fears.

—Cesare Pavese

When I was fifteen and preparing to embark on my first extended trip through an exchange program, news of my plan was often met with pursed lips and narrowed eyes.

"Russia? For four months? Are you crazy? Russia is dangerous!"

These conversations took place with acquaintances and relatives near my hometown on the East Coast of the United States.

"You realize that we basically live in a suburb of Washington, DC," I'd say.

"What does that have to do with it?"

"Right now, Washington, DC, is the murder capital of the world." This was in the early nineties when Colombian drug cartels were doing a swift business in crack cocaine in our nation's capital.

"Yes, but that's different," they'd say.

This was my first introduction to the complete lack of logic people use when considering the dangers of other countries versus their own. In any big city, there are dangers. And a person's likelihood of experiencing those dangers depends greatly on what parts of the city they visit, when they do so, in whose company, their general sobriety and awareness, and the businesses they patronize. Sure, I was pickpocketed on the Arbat, one of Moscow's most famous streets and a popular tourist attraction, but I've also had my car stolen in an affluent town in California. People have been pickpocketed on the Arbat since the fifteenth century. I choose to view the event as being a part of that history. Having a little money stolen from you is not the worst thing in the world. It teaches you to raise your awareness of your belongings and hopefully curb similar instances in the future.

Mike once left his wallet on a bus in Ireland. He got his exercise that day, sprinting six blocks to catch the bus while it remained in our Dublin neighborhood, and when he reached it, against all odds, he found that another passenger had turned the wallet in to the driver. The cash was gone, but the credit cards were still there. We had two choices at that moment. We could have been pissed off at the loss of about two hundred dollars (we'd just stopped at an ATM), or we could realize that we would gladly have paid two hundred dollars for the return of a wallet that contained a driver's license and a handful of credit cards. We opted for gratitude.

In Russia, there was also the gypsy cabbie who, upon learning that I was American, took my Russian friends and me in the wrong direction, stopped the car, put his hand on my thigh, and told me I could give him twenty dollars or get out of the car. I didn't have twenty dollars but probably wouldn't have given it to him if I did. My friends and I got out of the car, hailed another gypsy cab, and got back on track. Was it creepy when he put his hand on my thigh? Absolutely. But it could have been so much worse. Such scenarios and setbacks are truly minor when you employ a bit of perspective and view them in relation to all of the truly horrible things that happen right in your hometown.

Kidding, of course. I do not advocate anyone dwelling on their community's tragedies. What is worth examination is all of the good people who respond to such turmoil. It serves as a reminder that while bad things may happen all over the world, there are always good people who wish to help. As citizens of the world, it's up to each of us to decide on which one we focus.

* * *

When you tell people you're headed to Australia, their safety concerns center on the wealth of dangerous creatures that call Down Under their home. Sure, there are deadly spiders, snakes, crocodiles, fish, jellyfish, shells, ticks, ants, centipedes, octopuses, and sharks, but unless you go looking for them, chances are you'll see them only in the zoo or aquarium, if at all.

At the age of seven, Emilia had an unfortunate encounter with a jellyfish while we spent a month on Australia's Sunshine Coast. Fortunately, it was not the famous and feared box jellyfish but a more innocuous variety. We deduced this from the progression of "My leg really itches" to "My leg really hurts" with the accompaniment of just a few tears. The presence of lifeguard stations made this an easy fix. Emilia sat in the lifeguard's shade tent with an ice pack on her leg. She quickly forgot the pain and told the lifeguard, a middle-aged woman of exceeding kindness and endless patience, everything she knew about wilderness survival.

"If you're in an area with tigers," Emilia advised, "wear a mask on the back of your head because tigers like to attack from behind, and this might scare them off."

"I will absolutely do that," the lifeguard agreed.

"If you're going on a pirate adventure, take some apples and oranges in your pockets, because sometimes pirates get this terrible disease, but you will be healthy to escape."

I couldn't be sure but thought maybe this was a reference to scurvy.

"Right." The lifeguard nodded.

"If a cobra bites you," Emilia continued, "don't panic. If you panic too much, the venom spreads around your body. Don't panic and go to the nearest hospital."

"Good to know. Thanks for that," the lifeguard said.

"If you know you're going into cobra territory," Emilia continued, with apparently more knowledge to impart, "make friends with a mongoose. The poison doesn't affect mongooses, and mongooses eat cobras."

"Right, got it."

"If you're driving in a car through the desert and a sandstorm comes, stay inside the car. When a sandstorm comes, when the sand hits your skin, it feels like tiny, sharp rocks. If you're walking through the desert, go behind a rock or go inside a cave to protect yourself from the sand. If there's no rocks or anything to hide in, get out a shirt or a backpack and cover up your face."

"How does your leg feel?" the lifeguard asked.

"Good," Emilia said, removing the ice pack and exhausted of survival knowledge for the time being.

I hadn't heard of an ice pack as a remedy for jellyfish stings (or Portuguese man-of-war, as may have been the case), but it seemed to work well. I was grateful for the lifeguard's knowledge, as left alone I might have panicked and used the old, supposed remedy of urinating on my child, which would no doubt have scarred her far worse than the jellyfish sting.

It turns out that urine may actually trigger the release of more venom and is not thought to be a suitable reaction to caring for a victim. Vinegar is preferred, and on some beaches in Australia, you can find vinegar stations, where a pot of vinegar sits waiting for anyone who might need it. An accompanying sign reads:

> *Vinegar. For use on marine stings.*
> *Pour on—do not rub. Seek medical attention.*

When I later learned this, I thought it might be the sort of thing Emilia would like to add to her bank of survival knowledge.

"Emilia, do you know what to use to treat a jellyfish sting?" I asked.

"Yes, Mom. It's vinegar. Everyone knows that."

* * *

When you tell people you are headed to Brazil, their safety concerns center on violent crime. There is no question that crime is a problem in Brazil, compounded by extensive corruption throughout the Brazilian government and law enforcement, especially in many of the big cities we visited, like Rio de Janeiro, Salvador, and São Paulo. While tourists are targeted for bag snatching and pickpocketing, most of the violent crime relates to the drug trade. Just as in the

United States, a nasty crack habit will drastically increase your chances of being involved in a violent crime. This doesn't mean that my crack-free status lessens my vigilance in staying safe. In big cities and crowded areas, I keep my children close at all times.

"Ivy, you have to stay with me, and you have to hold my hand," I told her, as Mike had a similar conversation with Emilia ahead of us. We made our way along the narrow streets of Salvador's historic Pelourinho area.

"But *why*, Mom?" Ivy asked. "*Why* do I always have to hold your hand?"

"You don't always have to hold my hand," I said. "But you do now because of the crowds of people and the bumpy streets." Both girls struggled with the word *cobblestone* and had reverted to *bumpy streets* as a substitute.

"But, Mom, I'm not going to trip or get lost. I *promise*."

"I know you won't, Ivy, and I believe you. But I'm afraid I might fall down or get lost. So I need you to help me stay safe."

With this, a satisfactory explanation, Ivy puffed up her chest, held my hand tighter, and walked with determination. "Don't worry, Mom," she said, "I'll keep you safe."

Mike's parents, visiting us for part of our Brazilian adventure, followed behind as the six of us made our way to a row of restaurants and sat at an outdoor table. We ordered drinks and food, and our waiter placed the slip of paper with our written requests into a basket at the end of a long rope. After ringing a bell to alert the restaurant's second-floor staff, the basket was raised on a pulley system to the upstairs kitchen. We'd been in Brazil long enough to learn that the country is both delightful and an exercise in patience. The pulley system reinforced this, so while we settled in for what promised to be a considerable wait, my mother-in-law produced her cell phone and turned it over to Emilia and Ivy. She keeps a number of games on her phone for such instances with her grandchildren. Mike and I don't allow the girls to use any sort of electronics at a dinner table, instead forcing them into tense games of I-Spy or old-fashioned conversation, but we let the indulgence go since it came from Nana. The girls played happily while the adults chatted. A waiter approached then and began rapidly speaking to me in Portuguese.

"Please repeat slowly," I requested, unsure of what he was trying to communicate. "He wants the girls to sit on the other side of the table," I relayed to the rest of the group. Loud drumming echoed through the city streets. The waiter made hand motions to indicate people coming down the street. "Maybe the drummers are coming through here and we need to make room. I think it's a parade," I said.

"Ooh, a parade!" the girls said in unison.

The waiter looked increasingly frustrated with me. He continued speaking, and in my fractured Portuguese, I suddenly understood his meaning. He pantomimed grabbing the phone and running. Now it was clear.

"Oh, wait," I corrected. "Cancel that. No parade."

"Aw, man!" Ivy said.

"Why not?" Emilia asked. "Did we miss it?"

"He doesn't want the girls sitting on the side of the table open to the street. He's trying to warn us that someone will snatch the cell phone and run."

"That's very different from a parade," my father-in-law said.

"Well, yes," I conceded. "Yes, it is."

It was the perfect opportunity to reinstate our no-electronics-at-the-table policy, a good reminder to remain aware of our surroundings, and a sad commentary on my level of Portuguese comprehension.

* * *

Todos Santos is a small town in Mexico on the Baja Peninsula at the base of the Sierra de la Laguna Mountains. The town itself is charming, though so much so that the word is now out. It's no longer the closely guarded secret its expat residents hoped to keep it. And with the addition of a four-lane highway connecting it to Cabo San Lucas, it is easier accessed than it once was. But this is a good thing, because I traveled to Todos Santos many times before the new road was in, a journey that included washed-out roads, suicidal drivers passing on treacherous blind curves, and the occasional obstacle of an ill-situated bull.

It was an ideal, sunny afternoon in Todos Santos when my ears perked at the sound of tires crunching the gravel in our driveway. I emerged from the house and immediately shrieked.

"Oh my god, what happened?" I asked.

Mike had left our rented home an hour earlier to take three-year-old Emilia to the playground, while I stayed back with infant Ivy. They returned, sooner than expected, both wearing shirts spattered with blood. Emilia wasn't distressed when getting out of the car but then saw me and immediately burst into tears.

"I'm pretty sure she's fine," Mike said. "She fell on the playground."

"She just fell?"

Emilia buried her bloodied face in my neck and cried harder.

"She fell off a ladder and landed on her face. On the concrete."

The Mexican playgrounds we'd come to know were jungles of rusty metal and concrete, often accompanied by the faint whiff of marijuana. There were no such luxuries as soft-rubber surfaces, woodchip ground cover, or faux grass.

"And the crappy thing is that I was right there. I mean, I was *right* there," Mike said. His guilt was palpable, and I knew he'd beaten himself up enough already.

"Playground injuries are going to happen," I said. "It's not your fault. Is her nose broken?"

"I don't think so. But I shouldn't have taken her to that stupid playground."

"It's not your fault," I repeated. "What's on her shirt?" She'd calmed down enough for me to hold her at arm's length to survey the damage.

"Blood," Mike said.

"No, what's this other stuff? I see the blood, but what's this brown stuff?"

"Chocolate."

"Chocolate?"

"She was really upset. I decided the best way to see if it was serious was to offer her an ice cream. So I told her if she could calm down, I'd buy her an ice cream."

"Good thinking." The injuries were limited to a bloody nose and a cut in her mouth but nothing that an ice cream couldn't easily remedy.

As any parent knows, accidents happen and will continue to happen, regardless of whether or not a parent is *right* there. I was holding Ivy's hand when she missed the last step while disembarking from a bus in Australia. The middle of her back and the edge of the step made sickening contact a moment before she emitted a perfectly understandable wail.

I was *right* there when Emilia, in the safety of our home in Boise, was about to brush her teeth when she inexplicably fell and hit her head on the step stool. That incident required a trip to the emergency room and stitches, along with hospital staff's full-body assessment of Emilia to ensure that she was not the victim of abuse.

Playground injuries, missteps, and random falls will happen no matter where in the world we are. What I try to remember in such situations is that a child's injury is not the result of travel or finding ourselves in one particular country. We could blame Emilia's playground injury on the harsh Mexican playground, or we could recognize that a child's injury is most often the result of simply being a child.

When people ask us if we're concerned with safety when traveling the world, we answer yes. Of course we're concerned with safety, just as we're concerned about our children's safety when we paddleboard in Idaho, ride bikes in New Jersey, or take the Bainbridge Island ferry in Seattle. Safety is a priority whether home or abroad, but there's a difference between staying safe and letting fear paralyze you. I'm pro-safety but anti-paralysis.

Certain rules exist for safety's sake, and these rules I always follow. A good example is wearing a life jacket. I have never been too cool for a life jacket and do not understand others who are. The objections of "It's uncomfortable" or "It's too bulky" are not strong enough to counter the possibility of drowning. And those who claim not to need life jackets because they are strong swimmers have yet to demonstrate to me that they are also strong swimmers when knocked unconscious.

My mother-in-law has always been an excellent role model for Emilia and Ivy by wearing her life jacket right along with me. She and I donned our life jackets and helped the girls do the same as we prepared for a three-hour kayaking trip in Brazil.

"I think you should wear your life jacket," I heard her mutter to my father-in-law.

"I'm *not* wearing it," he answered, in a manner that made it clear his mind was made up and there would be no further discussion on the matter. To be fair, the kayaking took place in a shallow, calm river where an adult of even mediocre swimming skills could get by without a life jacket. There was no alcohol involved, no motorboats around, and had we been entirely on our own, I wouldn't have dared suggest he wear one. He's an excellent swimmer who has spent his life in and around water. But our three-hour tour was a guided one, and a moment after declaring that he would not be wearing a life jacket, our guide instructed everyone to put on a life jacket. My father-in-law grudgingly did so.

The most important safety rules are to stay alert and aware of one's surroundings and to stay sober. For the most part. I make no apologies for my wine consumption. My husband and I enjoy sampling local drinks, and my in-laws have never been ones to shy away from an offered beverage. That said, there is a time and a place for indulgence. Getting *wasted* is no longer in my repertoire, and the majority of my wine consumption is now delayed for the evening hours when everyone is home with no plans to venture out again until the following day.

The six of us—my in-laws, husband, children, and I—were on Rio's Copacabana Beach on New Year's Eve, having spent the entire day there. We'd consumed caipirinhas throughout the day and early evening, but many hours remained before the midnight firework show. I'm sure each of the adults would have loved to have another cocktail. But with children, drunkenness already around us, and the prospect of ever-thickening crowds, we each made the unacknowledged decision to forgo *just one more* and keep our wits intact.

One final note on safety is having some idea of how to reach help if the need arises. When we're in a new location, I don't research the location of the hospital and the quickest route there. I do, however, immediately take stock of half a dozen people I could ask for help and reach with only a moment's notice. These can include neighbors, security guards, store clerks, and of course emergency officials. That information, along with the reminder that good people abound, is a safety plan that works worldwide.

* * *

In the Unlikely Event of an Emergency

*You know, all that really matters is that the people you love
are happy and healthy. Everything else is just sprinkles
on the sundae.*

—Paul Walker

"Mike, why are you limping?" I asked during our stint in Vanuatu.

"Oh, I just have a little cut on my foot," he answered.

The next day, I repeated the question and received the same response.

"Let me see this cut on your foot," I said after four days. When I watched him walk, it reminded me of when he'd broken his leg and ankle in a horrific rugby accident. This seemed more severe than a minor wound.

"No, it's fine," he answered. "You don't want to see it; it's not a big deal."

Two weeks later, I finally had the pleasure of looking at the bottom of his foot, which proved my suspicion that he had been downplaying the situation. The skin on the pad of his foot and the underside of his toes was, quite simply, missing.

The raw, oozing flesh that remained, along with the fact that Mike had been walking on it for so long, made me shudder.

The reason Mike's foot progressed to such a dire state had nothing to do with flesh-eating bacteria or lack of competent medical care but his own stubborn reluctance to deal with the issue while it was still a manageable one. Part of the treatment for Mike's foot was to simply expose the wound to the open air so that it might have an opportunity to heal. You'd think that there would be no easier instructions to follow, but this was problematic in Vanuatu, owing to the voracity of the flies. Vanuatu flies view cuts and scratches on human flesh like an all-you-can-eat steak and lobster buffet. They are not deterred by mere bandages but will swarm over whatever covers the delectable area and try to crawl underneath it. Some of my coworkers were unfazed by this. If I glanced down at a bandaged cut on my leg, however, to find a herd of large black flies struggling to burrow their way underneath my Band-Aid and into my flesh, I would immediately begin swatting manically at them and then wrap my injury in something more impenetrable, such as duct tape. It is not the sort of place where you want to have a large, open wound, and Mike was confined indoors in fly-free rooms for a few days to allow his foot to begin healing.

I tried to keep the carnivorous flies from bothering me by reminding myself that maggots have been used to debride necrotic wounds since ancient history. Maggots have saved lives in their ability to clean a wound far better than a human can. Maybe the flies weren't bloodthirsty; maybe they were laying their eggs in an effort to help, so that their little larvae could feast on the nasty bits and aid in the healing process. Then again, I was pretty sure not all maggots were healers, and I wasn't knowledgeable enough about fly species to know whether the Vanuatu hordes would help or harm. I stocked up on duct tape.

Now, when Mike tells me something is "fine," I don't believe him.

The experience was good preparation for parenthood, as when my children give me their assessment of an injury, I don't believe them either and insist on viewing the problem myself. One day they will follow in their father's painful footsteps, declaring that an impending infection is fine, while the next day they might demand Band-Aids for the treatment of miniscule cuts, imaginary wounds, and freckles. When the injuries are obviously of the contrived variety, I suggest the maggot treatment, but they have yet to take me up on the offer.

When we set up our temporary life in the Pueblo Mágico of Todos Santos for a few months (two years after Emilia's playground incident), one of our favorite activities was participating in the release of baby sea turtles. Tortugueros Las Playitas is a conservation group with a focus on the critically endangered leatherback, though they work to protect the populations of Olive Ridley and black turtles as well. Volunteers relocate turtle nests to an incubation greenhouse, where the nests are protected and the sand temperature is optimal. When temperatures drop below a certain level, common in the fall and winter nests, the hatchlings experience higher rates of dwarfism, blindness, crooked beaks, and other malformations. I'm not sure how you determine that a baby sea turtle is blind, but it can be done. Survival for these creatures is tough enough as it is, and I'm sure dwarfism or a crooked beak doesn't help.

When the nests hatch, the public is invited in at no charge. My adoration of viewing baby sea turtle nests is always tempered by my fear that an unaware attendee will mistakenly step on a nest. I've seen this *almost* happen on many occasions, and each time I'm a second away from tackling the unsuspecting human just before he (or she) realizes the destruction about to occur and corrects his footing accordingly. The only time I've had to physically intervene on behalf of hatchlings was when the person about to crush a nest was one of my children.

Volunteers are on hand to answer questions (How *do* you determine if a baby sea turtle is blind?) and to collect data on each turtle. After the turtles are counted, weighed, and measured, they are shepherded down to the shoreline. This is done at dusk so that predators in the sky have a harder time viewing their potential prey on the beach. Everyone is given a turtle to place before an unblemished stretch of sand leading to the water. The turtles are tiny, and getting delayed in a footprint or tire tread does not increase their chances of survival.

Releasing a baby sea turtle is an endearing activity, and watching it head for the water and battle determinedly against oncoming waves to make its way to the sea is a testament to the power of instinct. It's a fantastic activity for kids, unless your child's particular turtle is picked off by a seagull before reaching the sea. Emotional crisis ensues. It becomes an evening of tears and extensive discussion about the circle of life. You watch *The Lion King*, ply the kids with treats, and try to move on.

After one such evening, when everyone had calmed and gone to bed, Ivy woke up wheezing. For a moment, I thought we were having a relapse of grief for the lost sea turtle, but I soon realized it was something more. This was when I learned that, of all that Todos Santos has to offer, the medical clinics are paramount. Because excellent street food and memorable wildlife experiences have no meaning if your child is having trouble breathing.

It was the first of half a dozen middle-of-the-night trips to the Todos Santos emergency clinic when Ivy would wake wheezing. The first visit was difficult, involving a substantial language barrier and a game of charades in which I imitated the various symptoms of my three-year-old. I also had the difficulty of communicating that Ivy's voice was not a symptom. From the time she could talk through age four, Ivy possessed what can only be described as a smoker's voice. I swear, my toddler had never touched a Marlboro, but for some reason her voice during those years held a raspy, almost bluesy quality on which people continually remarked. The Mexican medical staff initially took this as an indication of sore throat, but after repeatedly pointing to my daughter's throat, croaking, and saying "nor*mal*, nor*mal*" they came to understand. Either that or they thought I was high. In any case, the trips became easier in time. We learned which window to knock on to wake the medical staff, who would then rouse themselves and unlock the front door. Ivy never showed dismay at the conditions of the clinic or the fact that the staff was always asleep when we arrived. This was an excellent example of the benefit of seeing something through a child's eyes. While adults might scoff at what appeared to be less-than-sterile conditions, or question the credentials of medical workers as compared to one's family doctor in the United States, my three-year-old daughter recognized that the Todos Santos clinic was a place where people roused themselves from sleep in the middle of the night to do everything they could to make her better. And they did. They administered breathing treatments, prescribed medicines, and came to know us well during our three months there.

I never felt in any position to doubt or question the medical staff. Desperation, especially from a parent concerned for the welfare of her child, will lead a person to believe anything she is told in the hopes of a favorable outcome. I know logically that desperation can be dangerous, as I can look back on a number of instances in US hospitals where I had every right to both doubt and question medical staff, but desperation and timidity kept me silent. I feel extremely lucky to have interacted with the staff of the Todos Santos clinic, as I believe there was no need for doubt or question, when all was said and done. Their care was exceptional, thoughtful, and appreciated.

"Make sure," a young, English-speaking doctor told me on visit five or six, "that you keep her away from the roads."

I understood what she meant. While the downtown area of Todos Santos is paved, the neighborhood in which we lived had only dirt roads. Passing cars stirred the dry, dusty earth into the air, and exposure to this was likely exacerbating Ivy's condition. I related this to Mike when Ivy and I returned home just before dawn.

"No more dune buggy," Mike said.

We'd rented a neighbor's ancient truck during our stay, but I often borrowed my in-laws' open-topped dune buggy to drive the kids to school.

"Oh, crap. You're right," I said. "I've been unknowingly filling our daughters' lungs with dirt twice a day."

"Yeah," he agreed. "That probably hasn't been helping."

Ivy would eventually outgrow her asthmatic inclinations, while I'm still plagued by dune-buggy guilt.

Though Emilia avoided the clinic on that particular trip, she'd been a patient herself a few years prior. At eight months old, we left her in the care of Mike's parents in Todos Santos while we drove to nearby Cabo to spend two nights with visiting friends. It was the first time in motherhood that I'd spent a night away from my child. I'm fully aware that scores of mothers don't spend a night away from their child until the kid is ready for their first sleepover, at which point the parent wrings her hands in anguish at the separation. I'm not that type of mother, nor have I ever pretended to be.

"She feels kind of warm," I told my mother-in-law before we left. "I just gave her some Tylenol, but maybe keep an eye on her." I left children's Tylenol, ibuprofen, and a thermometer.

"Boy, have these things come a long way," my mother-in-law said, holding up the thermometer.

"No kidding," I agreed. The thermometer was the type placed unobtrusively in the ear for a few seconds, and though neither of us gave voice to it, we both silently compared the device to the rectal variety and were thankful for the technological advancement.

Mike and I said goodbye, and I tried to ignore the ache of leaving a child overnight for the first time.

"Everything will be fine," Mike said, reading my mind.

"I know."

We drove to the airport in San Jose del Cabo, greeted our friends as they arrived, then journeyed on to a condo in Cabo San Lucas. That night, before hitting the town for dinner, drinks, and dancing, I called my mother-in-law for an update.

"Yeah, she's still a little warm and pretty cranky, but we'll be just fine. You kids have fun."

"What's her temperature?" I asked.

"Just ninety-nine. We'll be fine," she repeated. "You guys go have fun."

We did so, returning to the condo late. "Do you think I should call again and check on Emilia?" I asked Mike.

"No, it's pretty late. Let's just call in the morning."

At first light, I picked up the phone.

"How's everything going?"

"Well, we had a pretty rough night," my mother-in-law conceded. "She has a bit of a temperature."

"What is it?"

"One-oh-three."

"A hundred and three? Are you kidding me?"

"No," said my mother-in-law, sounding as calm as ever, no doubt for my benefit.

"Holy crap. We're coming back."

"Okay," she agreed. "So, I'll go ahead and take her into the clinic and just meet you guys there."

We apologized profusely to our friends for abandoning them a night early, but they had children themselves (older and in the care of grandparents in the United States), and they understood our plight. The drive back to Todos Santos was filled with worry, but we met Emilia and Mike's mom at the clinic, where I'd never been so thankful to have a cranky baby in my arms. With the same care and patience I'd come to appreciate years later with Ivy, the staff eased my daughter's pain and made the world right again.

Occasional sickness can't be avoided. Parents are adept at dealing with children's illnesses, but doing so in a foreign country often increases our stress and makes us question our need to travel. If one of my daughters has a temperature of 103 in the United States, I will address the fever immediately but without the same sense of panic that I do in other countries. I don't doubt the competence of the medical staff, and I know that language barriers can be overcome, but there's still the nagging worry that I've caused the sickness or worsened its implications by dragging my kids beyond the borders of their home country. In such situations, I remind myself that two important components of successful travel (in both sickness and in health) are a sense of calm and a faith in the people with whom we interact. In all of our travels, that faith has never been given in error. With that mind-set in place, supplemented by the occasional prescription, we're able to rest, heal, and move forward.

* * *

Remote Working

I don't like the word "balance." To me, that somehow conjures up
conflict between work and family . . . as long as we think of these things
as conflicting, we will never have happiness. True happiness
comes from integration . . . of work, family, self, community.

—Padmasree Warrior

"It must be nice," a friend said, shaking her head. She was referring to our time abroad, to the idea of spending months in an exotic location somewhere in the world.

"It is," I said.

"But we do *work* every day," Mike added. He constantly battles the perception that we spend all of our time overseas drinking booze out of coconuts on a beach somewhere while our children build sandcastles.

"Sure," she nodded. "All that work."

We've had the conversation a dozen times. And the people who have talked about our work with a roll of the eyes and air quotes have not meant to be condescending. But their assumption is often that in the States, Mike works full-time, and overseas he works part-time. In reality, in the States, Mike works about eighty hours per week. Overseas, he has a shot of getting it down to forty. But he'll still wake at four or five in the morning to get eight hours in before we venture out. And while it's true that we've done plenty of lounging on a beach, it's also worth noting that the dues were sufficiently paid by the time we got there.

To facilitate work, we often search for some means of occupying our children. This doesn't mean we pawn them off on someone or something else the whole time but rather that we make sure we have meaningful and healthy interaction with them *before* we pawn them off on someone or something (television) else. In New Jersey, we developed the morning routine of packing a breakfast picnic and then riding bikes along the boardwalk into Atlantic City. We'd find a quiet spot to eat bagels and bananas, drink coffee and chocolate milk, and watch rabbits frolicking under the boardwalk. I thought the term *beach bunny* could only refer to a cute girl on a beach, but this is not so, as evidenced by the fluffles of rabbits hanging out at the Jersey Shore. (You could also describe them as colonies, nests, or warrens of rabbits, but I prefer fluffles.)

"Ooh, Mom, let's go to that place," Ivy said.

She'd turned her back to the ocean and stared longingly and wide-eyed at the bright lights of a casino.

"That place isn't for kids," Mike said.

"But look at the lady. She's so pretty," Emilia added.

The "lady" she spoke of was a neon outline of a buxom and scantily clad woman.

"Kids aren't allowed in there," I explained. "They gamble in there, and that's only for adults."

"Then why do they make it look like so much fun for kids?" Ivy asked.

"That's a very good question," I said, offering little in the way of a real answer.

Aside from our discussions of vice, addiction, and mental illness, our breakfasts along the shoreline gave us an opportunity to connect with our children before losing ourselves for hours in laptops and work.

In an effort not to turn them immediately over to the television every day when the workday commenced, we enrolled them in an art camp. It took place at an elementary school within walking distance to the home at which we stayed. Location was key, as we were attempting to get by without the aid of a rental car. The idea of walking somewhere always seems so refreshing. I picture myself shedding pounds with each step, becoming trim and fit, enjoying the outdoors, and breathing fresh air. All of this is complemented by the fact that the environment is exceedingly grateful. I'm making the world a better place, and Mother Nature adores me for it. Of course, none of this is true. Walking more than a few feet with then three-year-old Ivy was never an enjoyable experience and always carried with it the uncertainty of whether or not a tantrum was in the forecast. She viewed walking as torturous and evidence of our cruelty as parents.

Despite the unpleasantness of the trek to and from art camp with whining and moping, we thought art camp would give us a bit of respite and allow us some working hours, with something more constructive than placating the children with television and snacks. This would have worked well had we not learned, from both our children's reports and the teacher's admission, that "art camp" had less to do with art and more to do with television and snacks.

There have been plenty of trips when we didn't have a Montessori school or pathetic excuse for an art camp to occupy our children, but as they grow, we've found it less important to have an outside activity or school arranged. Emilia is now firmly in the world of chapter books, and Ivy will quickly follow suit. At least I'm hoping so. For my sanity and in the interest of getting any work done, my daughters must have something other than me with which to engage. Whether home or abroad, I find it impossible to accomplish anything amidst the backdrop of:

"Mom, are you working?"

"Are you writing?"

"Are you writing about me?"

"Do you need me to stop talking?"

"I'll be quiet."

"I'll just sit here and watch you."

"I'm watching you."

"Did you know that right now I'm watching you?"

"Can I have a corn dog?"

We see no point in traveling to a location simply to work nonstop, but we're also not trying to condense our work into four hours a week. For both Mike and me, work is something we enjoy, not something we try to escape. I could say the same about my children. I just can't enjoy my work and my children at the same time, and each is most enjoyable when it has my full attention.

Work for Mike is a little more complicated. I can get by with paper and pen, while Mike needs an Internet connection. He must remain aware of what time it is in the Pacific Northwest and has been known on occasion to pretend he is at his office in Boise when really he's out of the country. This is to appease clients who think he will be less effective if away from the office (if they only knew). He's hung blankets on the walls of makeshift offices to soundproof against crashing waves or tropical birds that otherwise might give him away during a conference call.

People who know about our travel plans often assume that our productivity will drop as soon as we board the plane. The opposite is true. To quell the fears of his clients, Mike works longer and harder at the beginning of a trip than at any other time. Instead of waiting for the panicked phone call from a client or colleague who is uncomfortable with our remote working situation, he is proactive in calling them. Once they see that he is still accessible, available, and productive, their stress abates.

The hardware of remote work often involves trouble-shooting, but with a little due diligence and practice, all technical obstacles can be overcome. Depending on your location, phones and phone plans are often cheaper overseas than they are in the States, and maintaining communication comes down to finding the right service provider. If slow Internet is restricting your workday, you may need to scope out the town and find a better spot to log your hours. As previously mentioned, another option, when renting a home or doing a home exchange, is to offer the homeowner money to upgrade their Internet service. There is often a slightly more expensive but better Internet plan available, which the homeowner will be happy to activate if you offer to cover the added expense.

One of the most important aspects of remote working is a conscious effort for efficiency. This means simplifying your workday and tackling the important tasks without letting yourself become distracted. Don't browse the Internet, get lost on Facebook, or play Candy Crush. This is nonnegotiable, and I've yet to meet a successful digital nomad (by successful I mean productive in work and actively participating in the culture in which she finds herself) who wastes her time in the aforementioned trivial pursuits. When you identify and eliminate the time wasters, you'll find that your workday will take half as many hours as before, but your productivity has doubled. Most of us operate in a firm state of denial when it comes to how much time we waste on the Internet. By coming clean with yourself and changing your habits accordingly, you'll make huge gains. One of the biggest time-wasters online is news, which people justify because it's *news*. We equate it with social education and pretend it's necessary in order to be a valid member of society. Unfortunately, most of the "news" we consume is worse for your brain than Candy Crush, because not only does it eat up hours in which you might have been productive or had face-to-face meaningful interaction with another individual, but it also leaves you depressed. News junkies who disconnect from media for a few days find that they are happier people without the negative updates of politics, tragedy, or celebrity gossip swirling around in their brains. And if they go back to their media consumption after a break, they'll find that little has changed in the interim.

Many people with professions that involve an online presence also maintain blogs. If blogging is an active part of your livelihood or a necessary supplement to it, then great, blog away. But if you're trying to write the great American novel, develop your thesis, or put together a business plan, blogging can be a seductive form of procrastination. I know a few people who are accomplished at blogging in addition to keeping their professional lives on track, but I know far more people who blog about wanting to do something, which they will never do because they are too busy blogging about wanting to do it. This is relative to all forms of social media, of course. In any profession where social media is a necessary component of promoting one's business, it's easy to fire up the laptop with the intention of updating various profiles, only to find yourself staring groggily at the screen, wondering where the last four hours went. This can happen anywhere in the world, but the disappointment you'll feel is greater when you waste such time in a foreign city, where you could have spent those lost hours engaging in the local culture.

In addition to occasional lying about where we are in the world, denying ourselves guilty pleasures that waste time, and focusing on professional priorities, another tactic that comes into play to keep our work lives rolling is tag-team parenting. We'll take three-hour shifts of parenting to give the other parent an opportunity to retreat and make some headway. Mike often wakes at five o'clock and immediately begins working. When the children wake around seven or eight, I'll make them breakfast, get them ready for the day, and begin schoolwork. By eleven o'clock, we're ready to switch. I take my laptop into hiding while Mike finishes up the lessons, makes the kids lunch, and spends some time playing games with them. In the afternoon, we've both accomplished what we needed to for the day and can engage in an activity or adventure for the whole family. By alternating responsibilities and using creative scheduling, we can ensure bills are paid, stress is managed, and the children don't watch twenty consecutive hours of television.

The key to successful tag-team parenting is to actively battle resentment before it creeps in. It's not keeping score. It's genuinely wanting to help your partner and encouraging him in the pursuit of his goals. None of this is applicable only to parenting and working while vagabonding with kids, of course, but if a family doesn't have the mind-set of mutual respect and shared responsibilities in place, then the family members might as well continue being miserable at home and refrain from spreading that misery throughout the rest of the world, because it's not going to get better on the road.

Not all interruptions to work have to do with children. An interruption to Internet service can leave a remote worker with a feeling of helplessness and impending doom. No matter how much you've vetted your Internet capabilities, there will always be glitches of one sort or another. Instead of freaking out or resting your head on your laptop for a good cry, it's helpful to always have a plan for what you will work on if the Internet is not available. For Mike, this might mean sitting with paper and pen to outline the elements of a new project or marketing campaign. Being adaptable with your schedule is as important as being adept at your job.

While we work most days of travel, we don't work all days of travel. We are not accustomed to taking weekends off in the United States or abroad and instead plan our days off around circumstance or location. In the Amazon, for instance, there was a block of days when Mike had to inform his office that he would not be available. Not by phone, e-mail, or carrier pigeon. Mike and many of his colleagues find this state of inaccessibility even more uncomfortable than the biting ants of the jungle floor, but disconnecting and reconnecting to find that the world still turns is beneficial. The rare instances when we don't work at all through the course of a day allow us time to focus, energize, and develop ideas we might not have realized if we'd stayed plugged in. The time off is often as important as the time on. And it doesn't hurt to spend some of that time off drinking booze out of a coconut.

* * *

Stranger Danger

Avoiding danger is no safer in the long run than outright exposure.
The fearful are caught as often as the bold.

—Helen Keller

"Emilia, what would you do if someone stopped their car and offered to give you a ride to school?"

"I would say, 'No, thank you.'" She smiled sweetly, as if pleased with herself for knowing the answer.

"No! Wrong!" Her smile dropped. "You would scream as loud as you can and run away," I corrected.

"Oh, right. Yes, that's what I would do."

"What if someone lost his puppy and asked you to help him look for it?" Mike asked.

"Oh, no! They lost their puppy? I would get some puppy treats and walk around the neighborhood and call for the puppy and it would smell the treats and come back and then I would give the puppy back to the owner."

Mike put his head in his hands.

"No, Emilia," I corrected. "If an adult tells a child that he lost his puppy and needs the child's help, that adult is not telling the truth."

"But why would they lie? What happened to the puppy? *Please* tell me the puppy's okay!"

Mike turned to me and muttered, "We have a lot of work to do with this one."

We had this conversation many times when Emilia was younger and nearing the age of walking to school without an adult. For years she'd longed for such independence but displayed the all too familiar and dangerous characteristic of simply being too polite. As it is, I foresee accompanying her to school forever.

When you have an overly friendly child, it's difficult to educate her about the existence of people who might want to hurt her without destroying her endearing innocence. As a parent, the issue becomes more troubling when you run a search on sexual predators in your area. Nothing is more terrifying than looking at a map of your neighborhood completely speckled with red dots signifying danger. It's a lot like reading the news; you soon wish you hadn't done so.

"Mom, I have a great idea," Emilia said as we spent an afternoon on the beach during our month on the Jersey Shore.

"What's that?"

"Well, there are many shells on this beach, as you know."

As you know sounds oddly adult from a child, but it's a phrase she's adopted, along with occasionally prefacing a statement with *Mama, hear this.*

"Yes, there are many seashells."

"I'm going to *sell* them to people!"

"Hmm," I said. "That is an interesting idea."

But she was already gone, approaching strangers and inquiring if they wanted to purchase a seashell for a dollar. She didn't have any takers but enjoyed the interaction all the same. Her entrepreneurial spirit is another instance in which we find ourselves torn between fostering her outgoing, independent personality and protecting her from those who might do her harm.

My own run-ins with strangers in the past few decades have been overwhelmingly positive. Prague was no exception. We spent ten days there (pre-children), while on a Christmas break from work in London. From our hotel, we would cross Wenceslas Square, which is actually more of a long boulevard. A large cobblestone area was filled with vendor booths, selling everything from sweet, fried dough (the Czech version of a funnel cake) to tourist trinkets. What I loved about walking through the rows of stands was that no one there tried to sell an item until a passerby first showed an interest. Nobody was pushy, and that approach to salesmanship is difficult to find. From our time spent in Mexico, I'd become used to vendors who only relented after exhausting a long list of enticing remarks, such as, "Hey, lady, you wanna buy my junk?" and "It's happy hour, so I give you two for one on real silver bracelets."

It snowed while we were there, and we watched people ice-skating in a small outdoor rink, like a quaint little scene that I thought only existed in cross-stitch patterns. There are a million sites to see: Prague castle, the astronomical clock, and Charles Bridge being three of the main attractions. There are guards who stand on small wooden squares outside major buildings. Just like Buckingham palace, they are decked out in uniform, accessorized with weapons, and a show of it is made when they begin and end a shift. Of course, they cannot move and are therefore subject to constant picture-taking while tourists snuggle up against them. I don't know why, but I refused to do this. Maybe I felt sorry for them, because I could imagine myself wanting to slap in the face the next person who stood next to me with a cheesy grin for the scrapbook. This is why I should never be permitted to work with firearms.

One of the first things we did in Prague was figure out the subway. This was no great feat, as it only had three lines, and we would only be using two of them. We could have skipped the subway altogether, but it was cold enough that being able to bypass a few blocks was worth it. Standing in the ticket line, I furiously studied my Czech phrasebook, then gloated for a full hour after successfully purchasing two weeklong passes.

After a brief subway ride, we reached our stop, disembarked, and made our way to the stairs leading up to the street. I saw a man whose posture told me he was preparing to speak to us. He held something small in his hand, presumably an item for sale. I darted around him, but Mike wasn't so lucky. I looked back to see Mike shaking his head no, but the man wouldn't let him through. *I guess they* do *have pushy vendors in Prague,* I thought. Mike pushed at the man, struggling to get away. *This guy doesn't quit,* I thought. I reached back around the man, grabbed a fistful of Mike's jacket, and attempted to pull him away as Mike continued to push the man from him. But then the man switched from Czech to English.

"I am a ticket inspector. I am a ticket inspector. I just want to see your tickets." What he held in his hand was his subway-cop badge (about the size of a quarter).

"Oops," I mumbled sheepishly.

"Sorry about that," Mike offered.

We looked at each other and chuckled; the inspector looked as if he were debating whether or not to run away from us. We'd practically assaulted the man for doing his job. It's not the only time I've overreacted and jumped to conclusions, which isn't behavior that I'm proud of. All the same, I wouldn't mind if a little of it rubbed off on my daughters.

People assume that a healthy caution when dealing with strangers is especially important when we travel. The opposite is true, in that being wary of strangers is far more imperative for our children when we're in the United States. When we're abroad, our children are always in view, with few exceptions like the Mexican Montessori school, which had strict procedures in place for signing children in and out of school grounds. There is never a time on a foreign beach when our children frolic in the waves while we doze on the beach, or go into a public restroom by themselves, or even wander the next aisle over in the grocery store. We continue to have conversations with them about strangers because these are good conversations for any parent to have with their children, but also in preparation for a few years from now when they are permitted a greater amount of independence when moving about the world.

The importance of stranger-danger education does not take away from what our children learn about strangers from firsthand experience. From their interactions with people, they've learned that strangers are overwhelmingly kind, complimentary, giving, helpful, and joyful.

On a flight from Los Angeles to Seattle, Emilia sat in the middle seat. Mike flanked her on one side, while a stranger, a young woman perhaps twenty years of age and traveling by herself, sat on the other side.

"Hi, my name's Emilia."

"Oh, hi." The woman smiled. "My name's Sabrina."

"Did you know that this is the third plane we've taken and after this we have one more?"

"Really? Where are you traveling to?"

"We're going to Boise, but we started out in Australia. We had to take the first plane from one city in Australia to another city in Australia, I forget what the cities are called, and the second plane took us from Australia to America. I'm American. Are you American?"

I was worried for Sabrina. She was trapped between Emilia and the window just two minutes into a two-hour flight. Surely, this twenty-something was panicking inside at the thought of my seven-year-old talking her ear off the whole time. She probably wanted to sleep or study biochemistry or read trashy magazines.

"Yes," Sabrina answered enthusiastically, "I'm American, too. What did you do in Australia?"

"I got stung by a jellyfish, but I only cried a little bit. Do you want to hear some survival tips?"

"Absolutely!"

For the next two hours, Sabrina and Emilia chatted nonstop, about survival, animals, places they'd been, and places they wanted to go. By the end of the flight, Sabrina gave Emilia her address so that Emilia might send her a postcard from a future travel destination. Sabrina was sincere, and I had no doubt that if Emilia wrote to her, she'd write back. My daughter had found her soul mate, or perhaps her future self.

While Emilia is outgoing, friendly, and inquisitive, Ivy limits her interactions and prefers to have Emilia lead the way in social situations. The one exception is for waitresses. Ivy routinely tells waitresses that they are pretty. This is endearing in itself, especially in light of the fact that she awards this compliment to many waitresses of varying appearances. As long as a waitress has something pink and/or sparkly somewhere on her body, Ivy will deem her pretty and tell her so. Nothing precludes this, not obesity, deformities, age, acne, or grossly asymmetrical features. This often leads to exceptional service once the "You're pretty" statement has been uttered, for which we're grateful. We have wondered, however, if Ivy's preoccupation with all things pink, sparkly, and princess-related might be her Achilles' heel, her equivalent to Emilia's overly friendly nature.

"Ivy, what would you do if a princess in a beautiful fairy dress stopped her car and asked you to get in?" I asked. I didn't think this a *likely* scenario but was curious just the same.

"Princesses don't drive cars."

"But just say they did."

"They don't."

"Would you get in the car?"

"No, because she'd be lying. If a princess was driving a car then she's not a real princess and that means she's lying to me. No way."

"What if," Mike asked, "the prettiest waitress you'd ever seen told you to go with her so that she could give you a lollipop." In addition to her obsession with all things girly, Ivy is highly motivated by sugar.

"That depends."

"On what?"

"Are we in the restaurant where she's the waitress?"

"No," Mike answered. "You're at the playground. What would you say?"

"I would fire her," Ivy answered. "Because she's at the playground when she's supposed to be at the restaurant. She's fired."

"What would you do if someone tried to pick you up and take you away?" he asked.

"I would scream as loud as I could and kick him in the weenie."

Mike turned to me and muttered, "Our work here is done."

* * *

Dealing with Children's Milestones

No matter how much time you spend reading books
or following your intuition, you're gonna screw it up.
Fifty times. You can't do parenting right.

—Alan Arkin

"I don't know. I don't think we should go."

"What? What are you talking about?" Mike asked. "We've been planning this for weeks."

We weren't headed to the other side of the world for months on end, and we didn't plan on working while we were gone. It was a camping trip, a few days in the Idaho wilderness so that Mike might escape his cell phone, I could find respite from my compulsive vacuuming affliction, and the children could exist for a time without television.

Idaho is a good place for this. It is the fourteenth largest state in America but the seventh least densely populated. It's not crowded, is speckled with mountains and rivers, and is bigger than all of New England, which was an astonishing fact to me. I grew up thinking that Maine was enormous. But that's because I grew up in Maryland, which seems like a jagged little piecemeal of strips of land that other states didn't need.

When camping, we *partially* succeed in our endeavor to temporarily escape phones and vacuums. Mike can search out a signal in the most desolate of locations to check his e-mail, and the lack of a vacuum only means that I spend much of such trips furiously sweeping tent and camper floors (in vain, of course, because nature will go where nature pleases). The children are the only successful ones; they go without television and do just fine.

Most of the time, the only hitch to camping is the disagreement Mike and I have over whether or not to tell the kids the truth about wildlife. When they ask if there are bears and mountain lions, I say yes. Because there are. Mike prefers to lie to the children and says that no such animals exist in Idaho, because he doesn't want them paralyzed with fear and hiding in the camper the whole time. We have yet to come to agreement on this issue. But in advance of this particular trip, I had a different apprehension.

"It's just, I don't know if this is the best *time* to go," I explained. "You know, because of Ivy."

"What about Ivy?"

"We're so close to being out of diapers."

The early years of motherhood contain scores of moments I reflect back on and wonder where my logic went. But when you're in the throes of potty training, when you spend a large portion of each day cleaning up human waste, you will do anything to avoid setbacks. And at that moment, I viewed the woods as a setback. Over the course of two months, Ivy had reached a tentative and tenuous comfort with the toilet. I feared this delicate relationship would be shattered by asking her to relieve herself in the woods while I held her in the awkward and precarious squat with which we are all familiar.

"Amanda," Mike said in his patient and placating tone of voice, the one he affects when he knows I'm dealing with irrational stress. "She's going to be fine."

"I don't know."

"Why are you worried about this?"

"Because this is what I do. I worry about things. It's kind of my job."

"Well, if you're going to worry about something," he advised, "worry about making sure we have enough alcohol."

"It was *one* time," I protested. A spontaneous trip one year had abbreviated my normal preparation time. As a result, I'd failed to pack many things, including pillows, coffee mugs, and vodka. Mike doesn't consume much vodka, save for when we camp, when sitting around a fire is lovely but sitting around a fire with a cocktail in hand is divine. Luckily, I'd realized my error before we'd descended deep into wilderness, and a minor detour to a liquor store had us back on track.

Despite my apprehensions about interruptions to potty training, we set out on our camping trip. Not only had I remembered everything, I'd brought a ridiculous excess of necessities, including baby wipes and vodka. I still worried that the trip might hinder Ivy's potty-training progress, but my fears were unfounded. Camping *accelerated* her progress. She found nature to be far more welcoming and exciting than our bathroom at home.

The weekend passed without anyone pooping her pants or encountering a mountain lion. The worst things to occur were a few mosquito bites, and we spent the time not only with cocktails and bonfires but also with hiking, games, and a scavenger hunt.

We returned to civilization grubby and weary but pleased with ourselves on the success of our trip. As we pulled into our driveway, I turned to Ivy in the backseat and asked, "Do you need to go potty? It's been a while. Maybe we should try."

"Yes," she said. "I need to go."

I helped her down from the truck, and she immediately ran to the middle of our front yard and began pulling down her pants.

"Ivy, no! What are you doing? We're going to go inside, on the *potty.*"

"I can do this, Mommy," she said, and she squatted and peed on the front lawn. After being encouraged to do so in the woods, she could see no reason why I wasn't in favor of her relieving herself on the grass when nature called.

Delaying a trip because of a child's age or upcoming milestones is always a mistake. There will never be the perfect time to travel, and you'll inevitably be wrong about when those milestones occur anyway. Most parents learn this with their first child, when they hear from countless other parents what is normal. There isn't really any such thing as *normal*, as we soon find out. While one child may get a first tooth at six months and learn to walk on her first birthday, these milestones can easily vary by months. The idea of a normal schedule by which a child will grow and progress is right on par with the tooth fairy, but don't tell that to Emilia, who will likely believe in the tooth fairy until she's a teenager.

As parents of toddlers delight in telling new parents what they are in for (which may or may not be true), so do parents of teenagers like to tell parents of preteens how things will be. I'm more likely to give credence to a parent who says, "All kids are different, but here's how it went with my child . . ."

than to a parent who bluntly predicts my future, followed by "Just wait, *you'll* see." The latter type of parent continually informs us that we will not be able to travel when our daughters become teens.

"That's great that you travel with the kids now," one such woman with teenagers told me.

"Yes, it works out really well," I said. I sensed a forthcoming *but*.

"Because you won't be able to travel with them when they're teenagers."

"You don't think so?" I knew from her tone exactly what she thought, but there are situations when you can tell a debate is pointless.

"No! It won't work. You'll see. When they're teens, they'll have friends they won't want to leave. They'll be involved in sports and clubs and activities. Believe me, this will have to come to an end. Just wait. *You'll* see."

"Hmm." I nodded slightly, ready to change the subject. My skepticism came not only from my desire to continue traveling with the girls when they are older. Nor was it solely a reaction to her condescension. There were two other reasons for not believing her. The first was that, by her own admission, she'd never traveled for more than a week with her family. The second was an example in the form of our close friends who moved to Mexico for two years when their children were entering their teens. They enrolled them in the Mexican public school system, where the children made friends, became fluent in Spanish, and successfully navigated a school curriculum far more intense than its US equivalent. Sure, the children balked at the plan in the beginning. But they assimilated and matured and are all the better for having had the experience.

Beyond these arguments in favor of continuing to travel, I have to recognize the flaw in the assumption that a family dynamic in one house universally applies to all others. One family deciding that travel is impossible does not preclude their neighbors from packing up and heading overseas. As long as we are healthy and able, we'll continue to vagabond.

When you enter the state of long-term travel, you find yourself rejoicing at milestones you'd never before considered. While slogging barefoot through mud for forty-five minutes in the Amazon, Ivy talked about the feeling of mud squishing through her toes. And I realized that we'd made huge strides, both figurative and literal, from three years prior when we trekked to and from art camp on the Jersey Shore. In perfect conditions, on level sidewalk, clad in brand-new sneakers, Ivy hadn't been able to walk a block without whining about being tired and hot and hungry and cold. She lamented our lack of an air-conditioned vehicle and claimed to be starving, having gone a full fifteen minutes without snacks. But there we were in the Amazon, sweating through tall grass and thick mud along a marsh above the banks of a river, where caiman (mid-sized crocodilians) basked in the sun. We were tired, hot, hungry, and thirsty, and though Ivy doubtless had snacks on her mind, she didn't give voice to it or protest the grueling hike. Her behavior was a milestone in itself, and one we never would have encountered in the comfort of our daily routine in Boise.

Our friends, viewed by some as reckless for moving their teens to Mexico for two years of junior high, had their own set of unanticipated milestones. These included the evening of homework, months into their stay, when the parents realized that their children, for the first time, were completing their assignments without the use of translation software. Another language milestone came when the children's fluency surpassed their father's. Even more telling than their acquisition and comprehension of Spanish was the first time they had friends from school come to their house for a visit. This was a milestone that signified their ability and willingness to assimilate into a culture rather than withdraw into the safety of the familiar. It's an example we'd all do well to follow and one that makes me suspect that sometimes *acting like a teenager* is a good thing.

* * *

"I did it, Mom! I did it!" Ivy shrieked, hopping her way out of the bathroom.

"Uh, you don't need to tell us everything that happens in the bathroom," Emilia advised her sister.

Ivy's enthusiasm was not dampened. "I remembered to put the toilet paper in the trash!" she exclaimed.

"Well it's about frickin' time," Mike muttered.

I elbowed him and turned my attention to Ivy. "That's great, sweetie. Now let's just try and remember to do that every time. Okay?"

"I'll try," she said, though she looked doubtful in her ability to do so.

It wasn't the first time we'd lived in a country where toilets were always accompanied by tiny trashcans in which to dispose of toilet paper. But correcting such an automatic action as dropping toilet paper into the bowl proved as difficult as remembering not to brush your teeth with water from the tap. The Brazilian woman with whom we'd exchanged homes had gone so far as to tape typed reminders (in English) on the walls next to every toilet in the home. Nevertheless, we all forgot on occasion during our first few days. While the rest of us acclimated, Ivy forgot time and time again, to the point that, if we knew she was headed to the bathroom, we would not let her go alone but stand next to her as she did her business, chanting, *"Don't put it in the toilet. Don't put it in the toilet. Don't put it in the toilet."* Most of the time this worked, though occasionally, even with us standing there barking instructions, she'd still drop it and then look at us with an apologetic, "Oops."

It should go without saying, but when staying in someone else's home, I do my best not to damage anything. Despite my best efforts, there are always one or two casualties, and when we return to our home in Boise, I also expect one or two casualties. A broken glass or toy, a mark on the wall, maybe even a stain on a couch or rug. Of all the things that I might damage in someone else's home, I sure as hell don't want it to be the septic system.

Ivy kept up the good work in the week that followed, lapsing into old habits in only one or two more instances. As much as we hope that shedding diapers means we're past bathroom milestones, that isn't always the case. Even so, we'd come a long way from peeing in the front yard.

* * *

Holidays Abroad

*Every Christmas my mom puts our pictures through the years
on display around the house so we can see how adorable we once were.
How sad is it that I peaked at age four?*

—Jen Mann, *Spending the Holidays
with People I Want to Punch in the Throat*

"A Christmas lamp?" Mike asked.

"Well, you know, it's kind of the same shape as a tree. And we're sure as hell not getting a tree."

"True."

It was early in the morning of December 23. We were living in an odd and dated home on the Tasman Peninsula, in southeast Tasmania, Australia. Our Christmas accoutrements included stockings, stocking stuffers, and one gift for each child, which we'd purchased farther north before reaching our current rural accommodations. Beyond that, we had a small, stained-glass ornament of a Christmas bell that a kind woman had given us on Australia's mainland. We'd had a two-minute conversation waiting for washing machines to finish outside of a campground Laundromat. She'd asked me where we were from and where we were headed, before disclosing her own itinerary. She and her husband were returning home after a final visit with a dying friend. "What you're doing is wonderful," she said. "It's wonderful." She referred to our quest of traveling with our kids, but I sensed that she also appreciated our casual conversation and that it wasn't entirely focused on death.

Hours later, she searched out our site and presented me with the ornament. I'm not sure she ever realized the impact of her gesture, but weeks after, in our borderline desolate Tasmanian location, we clung to the ornament as the focal point of our Christmas.

"I'll just put it like that," I said, hanging the ornament from a lampshade.

"That's kind of pathetic," Mike said. "You're not doing it justice."

"Well, I don't have a tree to put it on."

"How about this?" He took the ornament from the lampshade and hung it from the living room's low-hanging chandelier, circa 1971.

"I like it," I said. "It brings mistletoe to mind."

The girls trudged into the living room then, groggy and trailing blankies.

"What are you guys doing?" Emilia asked through a yawn.

"Putting up our Christmas decorations," I said. Then I corrected myself. "Decoration."

"*I* wanted to help put up the Christmas decoration!" Ivy whined.

"Okay," Mike said. He took down the ornament, handed it to Ivy, then lifted her up so she could replace it on the chandelier where it had been a moment ago.

"My turn, my turn," Emilia chanted. And we repeated the process with her.

I have never been accused of being mushy or sentimental. But at that moment, we were the real-life embodiment of the Whos in Whoville, happy about Christmas but without much in the way of material goods to show for it. We stopped just short of holding hands and singing carols.

Over the years, we've celebrated birthdays and all manner of holidays with limited props. I've cooked Thanksgiving dinner from what I could find at a convenience store, we've celebrated Valentine's Day with nothing more than hugs instead of creating thirty Valentines for classmates who will promptly discard them, and in Mexico, we've used the dried, center stalk of a century plant (ironically named as it only lives for a decade or two) with a few hastily made paper ornaments to infuse our "home" with the Christmas spirit. Which isn't to say that our daughters haven't had gluttonous and capitalist Christmases in their past. They've had plenty. They've woken to a living room blanketed with gifts wrapped and tied with bows, overflowing stockings, hot chocolate, new bicycles, and so many presents that my husband and I briefly entertained the existence of Santa, because we knew we'd be insane to have purchased the ridiculous multitude of gifts ourselves. But the other Christmases are better, when we don't have much but find that if we muster up enough excitement in our voices, that excitement becomes contagious, and our children find themselves celebrating just as much as if they'd woken up in Toys "R" Us.

As our two-month trip to Brazil approached, we realized that on Christmas Day we would have nothing for the kids. No lone ornament or stocking, not even a candy cane. We'd be in the Amazon jungle. All available real estate in our backpacks would be used for rain jackets and bug spray.

It would be our most adventurous undertaking with our children to date.

A month before the trip, I heard the girls talking about what they hoped Santa would bring them for Christmas.

"Just so you know, girls, Santa won't actually be able to come on Christmas." They stared at me blankly. "Because we'll be in the Amazon jungle." Both girls inhaled fully and then let out a perfectly synchronized wail. They keened in unison, mourning the death of their favorite day of the year, and I realized I could have better handled the delivery of this information. After twenty minutes, I was able to calm them down with assurances that Santa would figure something out.

"So, I kind of botched a Christmas discussion with the girls today," I told Mike that evening.

"Did you make them cry again?"

"No! Okay, yes, but help me figure this one out. What if we do an early Christmas? We don't tell them about it—they just wake up one morning to find that Santa came?"

Emilia must have had similar thinking. The next morning, we found a note on the Christmas tree. It read:

> *Dear Santa.*
> *Can you put are presents here so we don't have to*
> *carry them on our trip to brazil. from: the Turners.*

For the next six days, Emilia woke every morning, screaming, "Let's go see if Santa came!" and rushed to an empty living room. On Friday night, Mike and I stayed up late, wrapped presents, and arranged them under the tree.

The next morning, Mike and I woke around five, as is typical, but we agreed to stay in hiding. We wanted the girls to wake up and discover Santa's visit on their own. Three hours later, we heard screaming. We put our books aside and pretended to sleep as the girls stormed our room.

"Santa came, Santa came!" Ivy shrieked.

"Wake up, guys!" Emilia demanded.

We feigned grogginess and plodded out to the living room, where we had a delightful Christmas morning on the fifth of December.

I know plenty of families who wouldn't dream of interrupting their holiday traditions, and there's nothing wrong with that. Because of how we've chosen to live and explore the world, it is more important for us to remain flexible and approach each adaptation as a new challenge. Through trial and error (also known as making my children cry), we've learned not to discount what is important to the kids, but also not to allow tradition to confine us.

* * *

When Visitors Come Knocking

All journeys have secret destinations
of which the traveler is unaware.

—Martin Buber

"Oh god," I said, casting my eyes to the floor.

"What's wrong?" Mike asked.

"I just saw your father naked. Full frontal."

"Oh. I'm really sorry."

"It's okay." I shook off the image. "It's not the first time."

It was the start of the two-month home exchange in Brazil. We found ourselves in Londrina (Little London), a university town of just over half a million people. My in-laws had come to visit for a few days before joining us for a week's adventure in the Amazon followed by two more weeks of traveling a thousand miles of Brazilian coastline.

"He's just, you know, not real good at closing doors," Mike said.

"I know. It's fine."

My father-in-law is a craftsman, mountain biker, and master diver. He can harvest abalone from Alaskan waters and cultivate lavish gardens in desert climates. He can spot elusive wildlife, identify the healing properties of various cacti, and with nothing more than a series of guided stretches, cure back pain in someone who's been through chiropractors and surgeries in vain. He cannot, however, close doors.

Earlier that day, I'd walked by the bathroom door to hear the unmistakable sound of a man urinating. This is far different than the sound of a female urinating, owing to the difference in distance that the urine must travel after leaving the urethra but before hitting the toilet bowl water. To his credit, the door was *mostly* closed, and I didn't have to see him peeing, I just had to hear him peeing. And during the full-frontal spotting, the door was also *mostly* closed. I just happened to have glanced up at the wrong moment, when he happened to be positioned at the right angle. It was the perfect storm.

My father-in-law was unaware of both instances and will likely learn about them when he reads these words in print. Whenever I see my father-in-law in the nude, or hear him pee, or close the kitchen cupboards after he's fixed himself a snack, or shut the screen door he *almost* closed and wonder if any of the mosquitoes he's let inside are carrying malaria or dengue fever, I remind myself how enriching any venture is when they come to visit. I deal with their idiosyncrasies as they deal with mine, because the benefits cannot be quantified. My children's relationship with their grandparents has become stronger due to their shared experiences. They've released baby sea turtles together, fished for piranha, and logged countless airline miles in pursuit of adventure.

There are practical benefits as well. Two days before I caught a glimpse of the full monty, I found myself in sweltering Brazilian heat with a fever of 102 degrees, which is is not the most comfortable of states in which to find oneself. I was too preoccupied with weighing my chances of survival and trying to remember where my will was stashed back in the States to function as any sort of competent parent. But I didn't need to, because my in-laws were there. They fed my children and took them swimming while Mike was busy trying to convince me that my chances of survival were good (and trying to remember where my will was stashed back in the States).

A few weeks later, having survived São Paulo, Manaus, and the Amazon, we traveled to Rio with my in-laws and spent New Year's Eve on Copacabana Beach. This is a legendary beach party attracting two million people to drink and eat through the day and night, ending with a spectacular midnight fireworks show. Throughout the day, bands play on stages erected every quarter mile down the beach, while vendors hawk skewered shrimp, fried cheese, caipirinhas (the Brazilian mixed drink of choice, made from distilled sugar cane), dresses, ice cream, toys, cashews, and sweet tea dispensed from steel kegs. The multitude of vendors and the ability to rent chairs and umbrellas result in an environment that allows you to stay on the beach for as long as you like. The people-watching is never dull, with both men and women wearing very little in the way of swimwear. I was nervous about this and imagined I'd feel like an elderly, maimed elephant seal among scores of young, fit models in thongs. But the effect of Copacabana Beach on a woman's self-confidence as it relates to her body image is overwhelmingly and unexpectedly positive, because women of *all* shapes and sizes are scantily clad. After the initial shock wears off, it's just not a big deal. No one sucks in their stomach or tries to hide their cellulite. Everyone lets everything hang out, and there's something freeing about that (thought I, from the comfort of my full-coverage suit).

I had another reservation about Copacabana Beach on New Year's Eve; the idea of two million people on a beach was more than a little intimidating. And entering such drunken pandemonium with children in tow seemed out of the question. But because my in-laws were there to help, we managed to enjoy the festivities with our children, who napped periodically under sarongs until we woke them just before midnight for the grand finale. It might have been possible to manage the evening without my in-laws, but it certainly would have been more stressful.

Whether in Mexico, America, or Brazil, my in-laws have always been generous with their time and offer to watch the girls so that Mike and I have a chance to have dinner for two.

"Why don't you guys just go saunder into town, check things out, have a few drinks, have some fun," my mother-in-law suggested in Búzios, a popular Brazilian resort town.

"We should . . . saunder into town?" I asked, trying to suppress my smile and wondering how many times I could get her to repeat her mistake.

"Yes, absolutely, just go saunder around and we'll watch the girls."

"We might take you up on that."

"You should. Go have some caparangas (caipirinhas). Bossas (Búzios) looks like a really cool town."

"You know," I said with absolute sincerity. "You're the coolest mother-in-law a girl could hope for."

"Well, let's drink to that!" she cheered. "Who's making the caparangas?"

When it comes to visiting friends and relatives, we've learned over time what our limits are and when to give voice to them. We don't invite people to visit us, either at home or abroad, unless we genuinely want them to, and when you travel for months at a time, people will want to join you. If you are going to say yes, it helps to have fair knowledge of the temperaments, habits, and priorities of your co-travelers well in advance of the trip.

The few couples we know who have standing invitations to visit us anytime and anywhere in the world have a few things in common. These are not couples in which one or both parties make disparaging remarks about the other. We're not into the girls bitching in the kitchen about the boys and the boys hiding in the garage to vent about the girls. They are also not high-maintenance people; they don't balk at street food, can survive without hair dryers or particular brands of beer, and generally approach travel with a calm and appreciative mind-set. Paramount, of course, is that we all genuinely like each other and that they have some tolerance of children. My daughters don't scream or throw things, but they are children. Emilia is most likely to annoy you with her endless monologue of survival skills and obscure facts.

"Don't overexert yourself in the desert. You sweat; you die!"

"Did you know that the peregrine falcon is the fastest member of the animal kingdom and it can reach up to 200 miles per hour during its hunting dive?"

Ivy can wear anyone down with a single game of Would You Rather, in which her questions vary from saccharine to macabre without warning.

"Would you rather have a lollipop or a candy that's just like a lollipop but it doesn't have the stick so you just eat the candy by itself without anything to hold on to?"

"Would you rather have to eat your own eyeball or set your face on fire?"

My in-laws have long since learned how to respond to such questions (redirect by offering ice cream—probably all part of Ivy's master plan). When we travel with my in-laws, we know ahead of time what types of activities they will enjoy, which ones they won't, and the basics of what they need to get by. Part of why we travel well together is that many of our priorities align. We don't need fancy hotels, but we won't scoff at them either. Alcohol is as important as water, and we seek adventure but not necessarily danger. For the most part, we have successful travel with them down to a science. Once I learn never to glance at a mostly closed door, we'll be all set.

* * *

Language Barriers

If you talk to a man in a language he understands, that goes to his head.
If you talk to him in his language, that goes to his heart.

—Nelson Mandela

The quickest means by which I turn into a pile of goo is to be confronted by a child whose native language is anything other than English. There is something about hearing a toddler babble away in a foreign language that makes my knees weak. The children of Vanuatu have a little extra firepower in this department, as they speak Bislama, a language I find endearing no matter who is speaking it. There are French and English speakers in Vanuatu, but the predominant language is a pidgin. While the influences of French and English are identifiable, Bislama remains a language all its own.

Easily decipherable in print, Bislama can baffle a non-speaker when spoken. One of my first introductions to written Bislama was a sign on the door to the ladies' room that read "Toilet blong ol woman." I peeked over at the men's room: "Toilet blong ol man." At first, I took the *ol* to mean *old*, as if these particular restrooms were reserved for elderly use. I pictured handrails and mechanical toilet seats to lower the user, then catapult them back to standing when finished. And then I wondered where they drew the age line. What constituted old/ol? Was there a particular number of years one had to have lived in order to make use of these facilities, like qualifying for a senior citizen's discount in the States? Of course, *ol* didn't mean *old*, but *only*.

I would soon come to recognize *blong* as the most frequently employed word in Bislama. It can translate to *belong* but also any other word signifying possession or a relationship. Instead of saying "John's house," "house blong John" would be closer to the mark.

In the middle of town, a sign read "Pablik Laebri Blong Port Vila" (Port Vila Public Library). Most of the time, written Bislama was easily translated, such as "Kastoma Sevic" (Customer Service). Occasionally I would be stumped for a few weeks before the light would dawn. On one end of town was a grocery store called Au Bon Marche (French). On the other side of town was Au Bon Marche Nambatu. Figuring that Nambatu was someone's last name or something significant to Vanuatu culture, I didn't give it too much thought. It only took two months of shopping at this store to figure out that Nambatu was in fact Number Two. Suddenly my years of linguistic study weren't worth a single vatu.

On a poster regarding the impact of human presence to the surrounding aquatic life, I learned that a *sicucumba* was a sea cucumber. The rest of the text described how one should not try to make any contact with *sicucumbas* or any other creatures of the surrounding waters. To avoid experiencing any guilt over the fact that I routinely and compulsively poke at all sorts of things that would, could they speak, protest violently, I pretended not to understand.

My second favorite saying in Bislama is the slogan for Tuskers, the national beer (not to be confused with Kenya's beloved Tusker beer). While driving behind a Tuskers truck, I read "Bia blong yumi." *Bia* equals beer, followed by the ubiquitous *blong*. *Yumi* is a combination of *you* plus *me*. Altogether, *bia blong yumi* means *it's our beer*. I felt a special fondness for this phrase, as did many of my coworkers, for we had come to be quite familiar with Tuskers during our stay.

My favorite saying in Bislama was their version of "thank you very much." They are a thankful people, thankful for their friends and family, for all that they have, even if they have very little. The phrase *tankyu tu mas* is heard almost as often as the word *blong*. And it's rarely shortened to a mere *tankyu* but more often followed up by *tu mas*. It's hard not to smile when someone hits you with a *tankyu tu mas*. "No," I'd respond emphatically, "tank*yu* tu mas!"

Since Vanuatu, I'm convinced that the most important phrase you can learn in any language is "thank you very much." Not "please help," "where is the bathroom," or "we'd like another round." Learning to genuinely give thanks trumps all other concerns and has the added perk of inspiring people to help you find the bathroom or order another round when you so desire. Vanuatu also taught me to use the power of cute children speaking in other languages to my advantage. No matter how much assistance our family of four requires, when my daughters bring forth a "gracias" or an "obrigada," strangers are more than happy to step in to help.

There are times when communicating with someone who speaks a foreign language is easier than with someone who speaks your own language. When I was twelve years old, I worked a summer as a farmhand in West Virginia. I remember riding in the back of a pickup truck with another farmhand, a boy somewhat close to me in age. He was trying to make conversation, so he asked me if I was Ken. I didn't know who Ken was, and I didn't really care. My main concern was the distress at having been mistaken for Ken. Was it not obvious that I was female? Sure, I was a bit of a tomboy, but I thought I'd gotten through that painfully androgynous period where people told my mother what a cute little boy she had.

Equally distressing was the fact that the poser of this question was very cute. While I'd been thinking about how cute he was, he'd been wondering if I was some kid named Ken. I was mortified. The conversation was something like this:

"Are you Ken?"

"No . . . what?"

"Are you Ken?"

"I'm sorry, I didn't hear you." We were in the back of a moving pickup truck.

"Are you Ken?"

"I . . . I don't understand." I could see that he was getting frustrated, while I was ready to cry.

"Are you *related* to them?" He motioned to our employers, the farm owners in the cab of the truck. He'd been asking me if I was *kin*.

When we travel and someone says something to my children that they don't understand, they simply turn and stare at me for an explanation. In half of these instances, they've been addressed in English, but the addition of an accent to which they are unaccustomed leaves them dumbfounded.

I never thought communication would be challenging during three months in London. After all, I'd been raised on Monty Python. There were dozens of instances in which I longed for a parent to whom I could turn and stare at blankly until she decoded the situation for me, just as I do for my children. A shopping trip in London led me out of our hotel in search of a lint brush. I had a pair of black pants that attracted every piece of fuzz within a five-mile radius. If I wanted to wear the pants, I needed a lint brush, or at the very least a large roll of tape. During my stay in England, I had never noticed the people to be particularly linty, but they must be, as finding a lint brush in the consumer-driven community in which we stayed proved as difficult as persuading the average male that asking for directions will not reduce the size of his penis.

At the first store I went to, I looked around for a bit before approaching a store employee.

"Excuse me," I said, "do you have a lint brush?"

"Oh," she nodded gravely, "that's something for your back, right?" For my back? She looked at me with pity, as if I'd just told her of a rare and horrid skin disease that affected my back, and only a lint brush could cure it. Or maybe she thought I was afflicted with an exceptionally hairy back, and the lint brush would be used to brush my back. Other customers crowded in, waiting to hear the gory details of what it was that was wrong with my back. They were looking at me for signs of illness (boils creeping up from my collar, perhaps), then began backing away.

"No," I said with a little too much conviction, "I'm looking for a *lint brush.*" I pantomimed rolling a lint brush over my sleeve. "Something to take the *lint* off of *clothes.*"

"Oh," she said, this time much more casually. "No, we don't sell those."

I felt like such a leper asking for a stupid lint brush that I used ridiculously long and confusing descriptions at the next four places I visited. "You know what those things are, they have a handle and then a roll of like, you know, sticky kind of tape on the end, and you roll the thing over your clothes to take the little fuzzies off? Yeah, do you sell those?" Usually I got a nod of recognition, but nobody seemed to sell them, and I would then get directions to another store that might be able to help me. I didn't really need a lint brush that badly, but by then it was personal. On the one hand, I wanted to prove that there was a lint brush somewhere in England. Another part of me wanted to buy one, go back to that first store just like Julia Roberts in *Pretty Woman,* and say, "Remember me? You made me feel like I had some weird venereal disease that somehow affected my back. Well, *big* mistake, lady, because *this* is a lint brush!"

Eventually I found one. Well, not a lint brush but a lint brush roller refill, which by that point was good enough for me. I wanted to know what they called a lint brush in England. I figured it was like the difference between *apartment* and *flat,* or *elevator* versus *lift;* they just used a different word. When I was at the counter, I asked the checkout clerk, "What do you call these things?"

He looked at me for a moment, wondering if this was a riddle of some sort. Finally, he tentatively answered, "A lint brush."

"Right."

In England, I always tried to listen closely. I was constantly going over things in my head to make sure I'd heard what I thought I'd heard. I had a cold for a week or two during my first month in London. Mike told me I should go to a pharmacy (chemist) and get Dayners and Nightners.

"Dayners and Nightners?" I had to clarify what he'd said.

"Yeah, it's the same thing as Dayquil and Nyquil."

"But are you sure? Dayners and Nightners?" The names seemed a little silly to me.

"Yes, I'm sure. Pick some up today if you go out. You'll feel better."

Later, I went to the pharmacy, explained that I had a cold, and was offered Day *Nurse* and Night *Nurse*. That made more sense. I couldn't wait to tell Mike when he got home that evening.

"They're not Dayners and Nightners; they're called Day *Nurse* and Night *Nurse*." I held up the packages as evidence.

Mike looked at me blankly. "What did you think I said?"

I certainly couldn't blame all of my London misunderstandings on a British accent, as my follies had not been limited to speaking with Brits (evidenced by the fact that I couldn't understand my own husband). In a conversation with a New Zealand woman, we somehow got on the topic of when she gave birth.

"And it was just like flan, you know. Just totally flan."

I nodded dumbly but thought, *Isn't that a custard-like dessert?* I could find no way in which flan could possibly tie in with the rest of our conversation. *Is she trying to tell me that giving birth made her really hungry? Activated her sweet tooth?* I continued nodding and smiling, with no idea if my response was an appropriate one. After a few minutes of trying and failing to make connections between flan, mousse, crème brûlée, or even Jell-O and the topic at hand, I realized that she was describing labor as *full on,* as in *in full swing.* Neither flan nor any other gelatinous dessert played any kind of role in the birth story. I was grateful for that.

On another occasion, I sat in a London coffee shop where an elderly Scottish gentleman struck up a conversation with me. For all I know, he could have been telling me how his wife had just left him and he'd been told by the doctor that he had a mere three months left to live, during which time he would suffer excruciating pain. If that was what he was saying, then I must have looked like a real asshole sitting there nodding with a markedly unintelligent grin on my face. But he could have been saying anything. I honestly have no idea. At one point I thought he was trying to tell me that he was Canadian. Against all logic and reason, in a desperate attempt to take part in our conversation, I blurted, "You're Canadian?" He was obviously not Canadian, and this is quite possibly the stupidest thing I have ever said. I might as well have asked him if he was a puppy.

Navigating foreign accents and languages before kids was good preparation not only for traveling with kids but for parenthood itself. All parents experience a few years during which they must operate as constant translator for their toddler. Those years of training your ears to search for clues are, in turn, good practice for venturing back into a linguistically colorful world.

"But what if someone talks to me in Portuguese and I won't know what they're saying?" Ivy asked with her eyes cast down to the floor.

We'd returned to Sr. Zanoni's, a restaurant in Londrina where Mike loved the filet, I loved the salad with hearts of palm, and the girls loved the children's playroom. We'd selected a table adjacent to the kids' area, and I was in the process of signing them in when Ivy experienced a moment of apprehension.

"Well, you know how to say a few things in Portuguese, right?"

"No, I don't," she said.

"Of course you do! How do you say, 'I speak English'?"

She thought for a moment before mumbling, "Eu falo inglês."

"Perfect! And how do you say 'thank you'?"

"Obrigada!"

"Very good. I think you're all set."

Fifteen minutes later, when our food arrived and I attempted to retrieve the girls from the playroom, they didn't want to leave. Having a mere handful of phrases in their repertoire gave them the confidence needed to interact with other kids.

No matter how many phrases we teach our kids in advance of a trip, I don't think they'd be brave enough to attempt communication if they hadn't seen Mike and me struggle to do so dozens of times. By showing them that we try as best we can, they're inclined to do so themselves.

* * *

"Do we *have* to go back to art camp?" Emilia asked.

It was day two, and I hadn't yet grasped the full failings of the supposed camp.

"Art camp is fun. You *love* art," I said.

"But I don't know what they're *saying*," she complained. It hadn't occurred to me that communication would be a problem on the Jersey Shore. When we later dropped the girls off at art camp, I realized that it was more than just a heavy accent that impeded communication between Emilia and the teacher. Miss Linda, a heavyset, garish woman in her fifties, favored Ivy from the start. Her gross display of favoritism made me hope that she taught only week-long summer programs and was not an accredited teacher in the New Jersey public school system.

"Is Little Miss," she hissed, "going to do a better job of following the rules today?" Miss Linda saw nothing wrong with referring to Emilia as Little Miss and as if Emilia wasn't standing right there. Her demeanor implied that my eldest was a troublemaker to be watched carefully.

Miss Linda's speech indicated that she was Jersey, born and raised. She likely came from a long line of proud New Jerseyans. Compared to Emilia's speech, she had an accent but nothing more pronounced than speech that Emilia had encountered and deciphered before. The problem wasn't with Miss Linda's words or the accent in which they were delivered but in the obvious disdain that accompanied those words. The hostility Miss Linda directed at Emilia was a greater barrier than if they'd been communicating in different languages. Miss Linda's disgust rendered her unintelligible to my daughter.

Conversely, friendly interactions require no common language for successful communication. On a beach in Brazil, Emilia and Ivy quickly made friends with a girl who spoke no English. We watched the three of them play in the surf for twenty minutes before the trio ran up to where Mike and I were seated.

"Mom, this is our friend," Emilia announced.

"But we don't know what she says," Ivy added.

"What's your name?" I asked the girl in Portuguese.

"Jasmine," she answered. "Do they speak English?" She pointed to Emilia and Ivy. "I don't speak English."

"Yes, they speak English." That was the extent of our conversation, and the three girls clasped hands and ran back to the water, where they continued to play for the following hour. My daughters learned that, regardless of differences in language and culture, they can always resort to the universal message of a smile.

While an attempt at the native language of the country in which you find yourself is imperative, fluency is not. When you find yourself trying to communicate with just a handful of words in your mental dictionary, you gain an appreciation for language itself, but you also begin to understand the importance of body language, hand gestures, and facial expressions. With my index fingers placed on either side of the bridge of my nose, I can communicate to a pharmacist that I need something for sinuses. By learning the simple words "write it, please" in another language, I can bypass my ignorance of the numerical vocabulary. I will never rule out a destination because of the native tongue, because good intentions and genuine effort need no translation.

* * *

Let It Be Over

Never go on trips with anyone you do not love.

—Ernest Hemingway

"How many more days until we go back to Boise?" Emilia asked.

"We have about six weeks to go, Emilia. It's not yet time to start counting down the days."

"Are we ever going to have Christmas at home again?" Ivy asked with a quivering lip.

While my children are excellent travelers, that doesn't mean they don't have plenty of moments when they want nothing more than familiar foods, faces, and surroundings.

"I just want Australia to be *over*," Emilia added.

My daughters don't pine for the end of a trip when they are faced with difficulty. Neither one said she wanted to go home when we were slogging through the Amazon or battling a cockroach infestation on the Baja Peninsula.

Earlier in the day, before Emilia voiced her hope that Australia would soon be *over*, we'd visited the Underwater

World Sea Life Aquarium in Mooloolaba. They'd held thorny sea stars, viewed weedy sea dragons, and watched a seal and sea lion show. It had been a perfect day of childhood, with a literal cherry on top, courtesy of an ice-cream sundae to bring our adventure to a close.

When our girls experience this type of adventure, often fairly costly and designed specifically for the enjoyment of children, and then follow it up with complaints about wanting to go home, our initial reaction is to send them into time-out for being ungrateful twerps. Before we do so, it's helpful to examine *why* they are feeling homesick after we've just had, by all accounts, a perfect day. Sometimes the underlying issue is a wish to share these experiences with friends back home. We have a few tactics to remedy the discontent. One is for the girls to fill out their journals. They can write about the creatures they saw and the facts they learned, and they often draw accompanying illustrations. The act of writing down the experience is a form of sharing in itself and assures them that when they do have an opportunity to relate the occasion to friends, the details won't be forgotten. Another method is to have them draw a picture for someone back home, which is what Ivy did in response to the Mooloolaba Underwater World visit.

"I'm going to draw a picture of me and Jasper at the aquarium," Ivy said. "We're each going to be holding a sea star, and then I'll give the picture to Jasper when we get back home."

"That's a great idea, Ivy."

"And I don't know if this is okay to say, and I don't want you to be sad about it, but you're not going to be in the picture, Mom."

"That's okay, Ivy. Go ahead and just make this one about you and Jasper."

"Okay, but promise you won't be sad?"

"I promise."

"Good. Because I still love you, it's just that I'd rather it just be me and Jasper."

When writing in journals and drawing pictures for friends back home isn't enough, I open up my laptop and begin composing a letter to the girls' teachers. In Brazil, I typed away while Emilia dictated the following:

> *Dear Teacher and classmates,*
>
> *How is everything back at Boise? I heard it snowed on Christmas Eve. Back here it is hot. And it rains a lot. We went through the Amazon jungle which was cool and fun. We hiked through the Amazon jungle and saw sloths, caimans, tarantulas (big ones), and you can make a lot of stuff with trees, like ropes, bracelets, crowns, bow and arrows, birds, and other cool stuff. There are a lot of coconuts and mangos here. We drink coconut water and milk and one time we had twice a mango smoothie. What did you do for Christmas? Did you go on a field trip? Did you do a fun activity, like a party? I really miss you and Boise. I'll be back after Valentine's Day. Don't forget me.*
>
> *Fondly,*
>
> *Emilia*
>
> *PS: Can you please write back?*

I resisted the urge to add some clarification to "one time we had twice a mango smoothie," nor did I show any emotion when she told me to type "Don't forget me." By allowing her complete control of the communication, I gave her a sense of connection to her friends and class that was all her own. After hitting send, she perked up and was once again ready to enjoy the time we had left in Brazil.

Not every downtrodden remark requires intervention. It's good to recognize that complaints after a full day can be due to nothing more than fatigue, the same exhaustion that might lead to whining at home after an eventful day at the Boise Zoo. Sometimes, for both adults and children, the answer is as simple as a good nap.

* * *

"Vee go now!" Anna-Liesl barked. "Zer is notting for you here!"

"Sheesh," my mother muttered to me. "I was just hoping to look around."

"I know," I said. "But apparently *zer is notting for you here!*" I did my best impression of our guide without being caught.

"Oh god," my mother said. "Don't make me laugh. I can't take it."

I was fifteen. My mother and I were accompanying my grandmother on a meandering trip through Germany so that she might locate relatives. Our guide, Anna-Liesl, was a family friend. Well, she was a friend of my grandmother. When it came to my mother and me, we felt looked upon as intruders, and Anna-Liesl made it clear from the start that she was not overly fond of Americans *or* children. I was screwed. My mother and I were the unfortunate price she had to pay for a visit with my grandmother.

Anna-Liesl guided my grandmother, mother, and me through the clean, swept, cobbled streets of a tiny corner of Stuttgart. There is nothing tiny about the city itself, Germany's sixth largest, but with Anna-Liesl taking us shopping, also known as herding us quickly past a row of shops, we knew that our time in Stuttgart would be little more than a passing glimpse.

"Vee go now!" she shrieked again. My mother and I scurried to catch up to my grandmother and Anna-Liesl, for whom we were not moving fast enough.

The opportunity of traveling to Europe for ten days, where free accommodations and a guide await you, is a hard one to pass up. I couldn't be anything but grateful for such an experience. At the same time, my mother and I found ourselves spending the bulk of the trip gritting our teeth, biting our tongues, and counting down the days.

Anna-Liesl took us on many road trips around Germany. We traveled southwest for a brief glimpse of the Black Forest, which made me think of cake. The black forest cake I dreamed of was the American bastardization of the German Schwarzwälder Kirschtorte, which contains far more alcohol than its US imitation. Now, as an adult, I of course want to try the booze-laden original. The cherries on top of either version mimicked the Bollenhut, a formal headdress dating back to the mid-1700s in three Black Forest villages. The headdress included large pom-poms on top of a broad-brimmed hat. Unmarried women wore red pom-poms, and married women wore black pom-poms. I pictured would-be suitors scanning a crowded room for giant red pom-poms, while some of the wearers of those pom-poms tried to stand taller to be seen. Surely there were others who tried to be shorter, resentful of the bright beacon on their head.

When I wasn't thinking of black forest cake, I was thinking of German chocolate cake. German chocolate cake has no such relation to eighteenth-century German culture and is instead named in honor of American chocolatier Samuel German. The lack of lore didn't matter. I still wanted some.

When not thinking of cake, I dwelled on macaroni and cheese. Or grilled cheese. Or ramen noodles. My fantasies weren't lofty. I knew my mother was having similar thoughts. Our stomachs growled in commiseration. Every morning we silently struggled over soft-boiled eggs, striving to show respect and gratitude while realizing that we'd never before considered that eggs could be consumed with a spoon as opposed to a fork.

At dinner, Anna-Liesl served meaty stews. She'd dish everyone's plates, then say, "And ze rest for Gerhardt." Her husband would smile, his sausage fingers scratching the table, unable to hide the fact that he couldn't wait to dig in. And each time she'd say this, she'd give *almost* the rest to Gerhardt. But when the pot held the last remaining spoonful of food, she'd quickly move it over to her own plate. My mother and I tried to balance our appreciation of hospitality with our urge to laugh. Our host's hospitality *was* considerable. She went so far as to serve us a scoop of ice cream every night. I'd be so excited, until she'd walk around the table and douse everyone's ice cream with liqueur. At present, my taste buds have been sufficiently marinated over the past few decades to the point where I might enjoy ice cream with booze on it. But as an inexperienced fifteen-year-old, all I could think was that this woman had ruined a perfectly good scoop of ice cream.

We saw very little of Stuttgart. We missed the Schlossplatz, the main city square, nor did we visit any of the castles or Ludwigsburg Palace. Our days were scheduled to include soft-boiled eggs, countryside drives, rest time, the occasional walk during which we were not permitted to browse, and stew.

One of the countryside drives took us farther than the Black Forest, as we journeyed the four and a half hours to Dresden.

"It is not very pleasant," Anna-Liesl said. "Zer is little reason to go zer." This was a year after the fall of the Berlin Wall and Germany's reunification. While Anna-Liesl's Stuttgart neighborhood held the perfect balance of order, old-world charm, and wealth, much of Dresden still lay in ruins, and the city held the general air of depression that I would become further acquainted with when visiting Russia a year later.

My grandmother, however, had relatives in Dresden. Long-lost relatives. Her parents immigrated to the United States when she was a girl, before the war, before bombings, and before divisions that would make contact with relatives impossible for many years.

"Zey will speak no English," Anna-Liesl warned.

"Maybe I can speak to them in Russian," I said hopefully. I'd been studying the language for two years and knew that it would be my best chance at communication. My mother spoke neither German nor Russian and mentally prepared herself to sit smiling in a corner during the visit.

"Zat would be offensive to zem. Zey resent being forced to study Russian."

I didn't take Anna-Liesl's dismissal of my idea to heart. In any case, she informed us that she would be dropping us off for an hour's visit and then picking us up so that we might begin the journey back to Stuttgart in time for stew.

The family we visited included an old man, cousin to my grandmother. And I knew, with the rapid German gleefully pinging back and forth between them during our short visit, that *this* was the point of the entire trip. The chance to see this relative before he died (just a few years later) meant more to my grandmother than anything in the world at that moment. It wasn't about travel or museums or visiting Anna-Liesl (to this day, their friendship remains a mystery—they speak weekly, though my grandmother is always highly annoyed by their conversations). It was about the chance for a brief visit with a relative from childhood, someone my grandmother, for decades, believed she would never see again.

My Russian came into use, and the old man was delighted that I made the effort to communicate, no matter the language. He was elderly and poor and exceedingly kind.

That night, knowing that we'd experienced the highlight of the trip and that our remaining time would include Anna-Liesl's odd form of passive-aggressiveness and hostile hospitality, my mother and I lay awake, staring at the ceiling from a mattress on the floor.

"How many more days?" I whispered.

"Four. Four more days."

"We can do it," I encouraged.

"Four effing days."

"And ze rest for Gerhardt!"

"Shush," my mother chided. "Don't start me laughing."

Twenty-five years after the trip to Germany, my mother and I still burst out with the occasional, unprompted exclamations, "And ze rest for Gerhardt" and "Zer is notting for you here!" I remember these phrases when the going gets tough with Emilia and Ivy. If I can teach them to find humor in difficult times, they are not only more likely to get through those times with less stress, but we also create a unique bond as a result. I have no doubt that we will remember slogging through the Amazon for years to come. It was difficult for a healthy adult, and doubly so for a child. But when we reminisce about the fire ants and mud and piranha and tarantulas (big ones), we'll do so with laughter.

* * *

Mourning the Loss of Personal Space

*I'm drawn to the taboos that surround the human body.
I find it fascinating that we are repelled by many of the acts
and processes that keep us alive.*

—Mary Roach

"**M**om?"

"Ivy, I'm in the bathroom," I called through the door. "Please just give me a minute and then I'll come out and talk to you."

"Okay." Pause. "But, Mom?"

"Ivy, I'm in the *bathroom*."

"Okay, but really quick I just wanted to tell you three things. The first thing is that I want to eat an apple every day, so please make sure that we always have apples. If we need to go to the store to get the apples, then we should go to the store, because I want to eat one every day."

This made me forgive the intrusion. My daughters are big fans of sugar and all things fried, so I cling to any acceptance of a healthier diet as tightly as I can.

"That's great, Ivy. We can do that. You know, there's actually a saying about how an apple a day—"

"Except," she cut me off, "if I die. Then I don't need the apple a day."

"Um, okay."

"And the second thing I need to tell you is that I need to know if there's something weird about me."

"Something weird?"

"Yes. Is there something weird about me?"

"No, Ivy. There is nothing weird about you." This sounded like a fear born of chatter on the elementary school playground. "Of course, everyone is a little bit weird. But there's nothing *wrong* with you." By this point, I'd flushed and was washing my hands, long since having given up on the idea of using the facilities in peace.

"Okay. And the third thing I need to tell you . . ." I opened the door and looked down, where Ivy stood with an expression of deep thinking. "The third thing is that I forgot what the third thing was."

Most parents I know have had similar experiences. Your time and space are not your own, and that's just part of the deal. The only surefire way to have a moment's peace is to get the other parent in place to intervene on your behalf. When I approach Mike and gravely announce, "I'm going to the bathroom," he knows that I'm not trying to update him on the state of my bladder and bowels but that I'm asking him *not* to let the kids bother me for the next few minutes. This goes along with the tag-team parenting approach to working and is necessary for both of us to keep our sanity.

When you're on the road with your children, the lack of time and space to yourself gets worse. We've found ourselves in the tiniest of accommodations with our kids, from the narrow bunks of a cabin on a ferry to tents and camper vans.

As evidence of children's complete lack of logic, the smaller the sleeping quarters, the closer my children will want to be to me. On the ferry boat, where the bunks were two feet wide at most, Ivy asked, "Mom, can I sleep in your bed?" The idea was so ludicrous that I could do nothing but laugh in response.

"If anybody gets to sleep with Mom," Mike interjected, "it's *Dad*."

"No one is sleeping with Mom," I clarified.

In her younger years, we referred to Ivy as "The Night Fury" because of her refusal to sleep through the night until the age of three. As a result, we became very protective of the time and space in which we sleep, because we were deprived of it for so long. That protective inclination remains, and I'm thankful for it. Aside from the one immediately denied request to sleep in my bed on a ferry, the girls know that they are expected to sleep in their own bed(s) (they often share, depending on accommodations) through the night and do not attempt to crawl into their parents' bed at any time.

Sadly, I have no such boundaries in place when it comes to bathing. Vagabonding along the east coast of mainland Australia necessitated showering with my daughters in campground facilities. This included fielding endless uncomfortable questions about my naked body, impressing my children with my ability to put my face under the shower faucet, and longing for the day when I could again bathe alone. As the lone male in our family of four, Mike was exempt from any such duties. But we all had to adjust to being in one another's space twenty-four hours a day.

During our first three-month trip with children in Mexico, we arrived to find that our free accommodations in the form of a small guest cottage on my in-laws' property had no bathtub. It hadn't occurred to us that this would require any adjustment, but until that time, our daughters had only ever bathed in a tub. Showering Ivy involved much wailing, a combination of having shower water rain down on her for the first time and fear of the giant cockroaches that often stopped in the shower for a visit (and their immediate death). Emilia, at the age of five, was slightly less traumatized.

"Okay, Emilia, now just take a step back so that you're under the water."

"Okay," she'd say. With her back to the water, she would scoot back a millimeter so that the water barely grazed her buttocks.

"A little bit more, sweetie. Scoot back so that we can get your hair wet."

With eyes and fists clenched in an obvious effort to be brave, she'd move another millimeter. Using a pitcher of some sort helped, but showering was never a simple task.

Most of our trips involve seeking warmer climates, which is 100 percent my husband's influence, as I abhor sweating all the time. I sweat profusely anyway, and in tropical locales, *repulsive* would not be too strong a word to describe me. In addition to wanting warmer weather, my husband is also a beach junkie, and the combination of sweat, sand, and sunscreen necessitates frequent bathing. I try to relax on such habits, but it's a struggle.

As soon as we arrived at a beach in New Jersey, Emilia loudly announced, "Hey, Ivy, let's go potty in the water." She then proceeded to squat in a foot of water, pee, and proclaim, "Ahh, that feels better." The people around us slowly drifted away. I can't fault her for this. For years, she refused to pee in the ocean and would rather walk a mile to a smelly Porta-Potty than do so.

Later that day, I observed her standing in a foot of water, hunched over and closely examining her crotch.

"What on earth is our daughter doing?" Mike asked.

"I have no idea. I'll check it out." I made my way to her and saw a concerned look on her face, both hands firmly rooting around in the bottom of her swimsuit. "Emilia, what are you doing? Can you please take your hands out of your private parts?"

"I just have some sand in here," she said, standing and turning to face me. The crotch of her bathing suit hung a few inches lower than normal, filled with about three cups of sand. This is a faulty design in girls' swimwear; the crotch lining of the suit includes an opening on one side, allowing sand to enter and get trapped there. The problem intensifies when your child likes to sit in the sand and let the surf wash over her for hours on end.

"Oh, um, okay. I know what to do." I had no idea what to do. "Let's walk up to the boardwalk where the outdoor shower is. Maybe we can take care of it there." At first, I attempted to extricate the sand myself, but this was as ineffective as Emilia's own efforts, and more visually disturbing, as now it was an adult rooting around in a child's crotch as opposed to the child herself. "Okay, that's not going to work. You need to take the suit off."

"Here?" She looked terrified; people milled up and down the boardwalk.

"I'll tell you what. I'll wrap a towel around you, and you can take the suit off. Then I'll rinse out the suit, and you can put it back on."

"But what will I do when I'm naked?"

"You'll keep the towel wrapped around you."

Her anxiety over standing on the boardwalk wrapped in only a towel was endearing in light of the fact that she had no problem examining her crotch for all to see or announcing to the general public that she was urinating in the waters in which they frolicked.

All parents are familiar with having to address situations like these. The awkward moments you could never have predicted, which take a fair amount of troubleshooting to navigate, are plentiful. When you travel, you must solve these minor issues in an unfamiliar environment and often in areas where you feel you are on display. You have to sacrifice some of the space and privacy to which you are accustomed. In that regard, parents are well suited to long-term travel in tight spaces, because they've long since forgotten what it's like to use the bathroom in peace. As long as there's a working toilet, life is good.

* * *

Tight quarters require concessions of time, space, and privacy. Such situations are easily managed by focusing on the benefits. When we are all crammed in the same room, I am less likely to lose one of my children. We learn to get along, whether we feel like it or not, because there's no other choice. High-maintenance tendencies are eliminated, because *vagabonding* and *high maintenance* do not get along. We foster a sense of gratitude, reminding each other that, in many parts of the world, it's not uncommon for three generations of a family to share miniscule living conditions. Finally, tight quarters give us a positive outlook on the future, because as uncomfortable as our limited space may be, we take comfort in the fact that it's temporary.

* * *

A Little Culture Goes a Long Way

To travel is to discover that everyone is wrong about other countries.

—Aldous Huxley

Long-term, nomadic travel fosters compassion, adaptability, perspective, gratitude, and a sense of wonder. It would be both condescending and remiss to say that I've seen these qualities evolve only in my children, because they've also developed in me. Whenever I experience stress over how my daughters will react to a new schedule or environment, I'm quickly reminded that they are far more adaptable than I am.

"What time does your flight leave?" my sister asked over the phone. The following day, we would depart Florida, bound for Brazil.

"Ten o'clock at night," I answered.

"Oh, that's good," she said. "They'll sleep on the plane."

"Yes, although it's interesting, because I've realized that it doesn't really matter if they do or not. If they don't sleep enough on the plane, they'll nap on a chair in the airport during a layover."

They've napped by pools under towels, on beaches under umbrellas, on boats and buses, and during piggyback rides. They've grown out of requiring set schedules and now recognize when their bodies require rest and actively take steps to accommodate themselves. Being tired no longer results in tantrums or a refusal to persevere. I'm the one most likely to fall apart in the face of fatigue.

I've learned from my daughters that when communication is challenging, whether due to differences of language or culture, it's best to revert to a smile, though admittedly my daughters' smiles have a greater positive effect on strangers than mine does. The exposure to different languages has rekindled my love for the study of language, given my children an ear for language, and enhanced how all of us understand the use of our native language. Once Emilia and Ivy recognized the power of saying *thank you* in Portuguese whenever the opportunity presented itself, they became equally aware of the power of thanks in all languages.

Compassion and perspective go hand in hand. My daughters comprehend a world of varied cultures because they've been exposed to them. They understand that there are people in the world who live without electricity and running water, but they also know that children in such families are equally adept at hide-and-seek. Emilia's emptied my pockets of change to spread among the multitude of buskers on the street corners of Byron Bay, Australia, with the commentary, "They're all so good, Mom, but being a musician must be hard. I hope they make a lot of money tonight." Ivy's shown appropriate solemnity when entering a Brazilian church, with no knowledge of the religion herself but an understanding that it is important to others.

They've escaped how many of us were raised, confined by convention to a neighborhood, so that in the child's mind, nothing exists beyond their subdivision. They value everyone they meet, from the buskers and the churchgoers to the bus drivers and store clerks. As a result of the cultural exposure, when tempers flare and one of my girls stomps her foot, puts her hands on her hips, and declares, "No fair," it is only a moment before she recants and acknowledges how truly lucky she is. "Okay, that's not exactly true," she'll say. I never know exactly what or whom they're thinking of in those moments. It could be a remembrance of an introduction to poverty, or the internal acknowledgment that, despite the difficulties of the Amazon trek, their classmates in Boise didn't have the same opportunity. This sudden reversal in behavior, the acknowledgment of what they have and the gratitude it merits, immediately disarms whatever meltdown was on the horizon.

I've tried to follow suit. I now find it impossible to dwell on traffic after viewing, from the safety of an air-conditioned bus, a mother riding a bike with her toddler and infant balanced on the handlebars. A lack of hot water is no cause for complaint after touring the ominous ruins of an Australian convict site, where ten-year-old inmates both bathed and relieved themselves (and sometimes drowned) in the frigid waters of the sea.

Nor will I wallow in the negative after seeing all of the good in the world. Islamophobia will never make sense to me in light of the Moroccan woman who presented us with a bowl of couscous, motivated by nothing more than the desire to spread friendship (and excellent food) to foreigners. Government corruption is a terrible problem in Brazil, but I'm far more knowledgeable about the inherent desire of Brazilians to assist anyone who asks for help or directions. The good in the world exists and perseveres regardless of money or struggle or the mainstream media's perplexing inclination to ignore it in favor of something that will inspire fear and hatred.

The most delightful and entertaining perk of routinely exposing my children to parts of the world beyond their hometown is that it seems to have prolonged their sense of wonder.

This was perfectly evidenced in the Everglades. My inclination is to call them the "Florida" Everglades, but as Marjory Stoneman Douglas deftly pointed out with the opening line of her 1947 book *The Everglades: River of Grass,* "There are no other Everglades in the world." Florida is superfluous. With a long drive ahead of us, which would be followed by twenty hours in various airports, we decided to stop along the Tamiami Trail for a brief look at these unique tropical wetlands.

In the 1920s, Collier County's Ochopee area existed as a one-family tomato-farming community. It still lays claim to the smallest post office in the United States. At some point in the last hundred years, Collier County residents saw the potential of tourism, perhaps not long after the aforementioned conservation rock star Marjory Stoneman Douglas turned the public view of the Everglades from that of stinky swamp to an invaluable river. Today, visitors can stop in at any number of airboat tour businesses along the Tamiami. We chose Wooten's, highly recommended by friends in Naples, and because Wooten's is fun to say.

We asked if we would need mosquito repellant at that time of day, but the lady who sold us our tickets assured us that we would not. "But you do get to feed the fish, and maybe we'll see an alligator come over," she added, handing

Emilia and Ivy each a small paper bag filled with dog food. Behind the ticket booth, a wooden viewing platform hovered over the water. The girls threw handfuls of dog food into the water, and the fish swarmed in response. Within a minute, a ten-foot alligator made his (or her) way over to us and began chomping on the fish.

"That is a big alligator," Emilia said.

"Come and get your food!" Ivy called. "Sorry that you're getting eaten, little fishies."

A minute after that, a seven-foot alligator joined the buffet, and upon seeing this monster, Ivy exclaimed, "Look! A baby!"

When it was time for the airboat ride, we boarded in the front row so that the girls might have a better view. For thirty minutes, we glided on the water, spotting more alligators, each one as exciting as those before it, even if the gator we viewed did nothing more than remain very still or disappear silently under the surface. I attribute the mystique of alligators to a combination of human fear toward the reptiles and all the facts that make the beasts unique. Their reminiscence of dinosaurs holds an odd allure. Alligators have been around for 37 million years, and for that fact alone, they merit respect. (Although cockroaches date back 320 million years, yet I feel no respect owed to them.) Alligators are intriguing: they engage in group courtship, their sex is determined by the temperature of their nests, and they are born with an egg tooth to help free them from their eggs when the time is right.

Many hours remained before our flight to Brazil, so after the airboat ride we decided to wander around Wooten's park, which included exhibits of alligators and various reptiles, Siberian tigers, and a Florida panther. The facilities were in need of updating; as a result, my fascination with the animals and reptiles was tempered by my sadness for them. We watched an alligator show, where two men hovered over a giant alligator in a small pen and told us alligator facts. They cut up chunks of pork butt and tossed them over a fence into a large lake where more than fifty alligators vied for a piece of meat. Some of those who missed out hissed their displeasure. For our final experience with the alligators, Emilia and Ivy were permitted to hold a baby alligator with banded jaw, and each girl beamed as she did so.

We were drenched in sweat (which is not how I wanted to begin the twenty hours of travel ahead of us) and had been bitten by a number of mosquitoes.

"Let's get out of here," I whispered to Mike.

"Okay, we just have to stop and see the panthers and tigers real quick."

"All right," I agreed.

Emilia had asked the alligator handlers every conceivable question about the reptiles by that point, so she was ready to move on as well.

The Florida panther is an endangered animal, massive and sleek. There are one hundred sixty estimated in the wild. Human encroachment has reduced their numbers drastically, resulting in inbreeding, which has further damaged the health of the species. Our opportunity to view the creature was, for us, a rare occurrence.

"Mom, I like the panther, but there are a lot of mosquitoes," Ivy said. I looked to find her scratching a number of bites. Emilia stood beside her with a large mosquito perched in the center of her forehead. Without warning, I whacked her in the head with the palm of my hand.

"Mom!" she protested.

"I'm sorry, sweetie, I was just trying to kill a mosquito." I removed my palm to reveal a large smear of blood; the mosquito had been well fed at her time of death.

"You know," she said, "the mosquitoes are just trying to feed their babies."

"I know, Emilia, but I prefer they not do it from your face."

The Siberian tiger has a slightly more stable population than the Florida panther, with more than five hundred fifty estimated in the wild. They are more massive than the panther and have been known to attack bears larger than themselves in the wild. As we continued to sweat, staring at the animals, I wondered how a Siberian tiger could tolerate the Florida heat. It seemed the equivalent of someone placing me in the middle of Siberia, with the notable difference that I would quickly die, and the tiger in front of me was very much alive.

"Mom?" Emilia asked.

I looked down to see a mosquito feeding on her arm and quickly hit her there.

"Ow!" she protested again.

"I'm sorry."

"Can we go?" she asked.

"Yes," I answered, and as the four of us trekked back through the animal park to the gift shop, where we hoped to purchase some bug-bite relief, we swatted at each other constantly.

We reached the car, turned on the air-conditioning, and attempted to nurse our wounds. We made no other stops before reaching the airport, though we were slowed by traffic periodically as we neared Miami.

"Whoa!" Ivy said. "You guys have to see this!"

"What is it?" Emilia asked.

"It's a really big trash truck!"

"Whoa!"

Five minutes later, it was Emilia's turn. "Oh my gosh!"

"What is it?" Ivy asked.

"Look at how pretty that hibiscus flower is! I can see the pistil."

I looked to the right and saw, outside of our window, a hibiscus tree in full bloom. I wasn't sure how much of the flower's anatomy she could see from the backseat but smiled at her inclination to show off her floral vocabulary.

"That's cool," Ivy said. "But did you see the trash truck?"

On the same day that my girls held a baby alligator and took an airboat ride through the Everglades, on the day when they viewed an oddly paired Florida panther and Siberian tiger, they displayed equal wonder for a flower and a trash truck. That sense of wonder for all things is something we hope to hold on to.

"That was a really pretty flower," I said to Mike.

"True," he agreed. "But did you see the trash truck?"

* * *

Choosing the Next Trip

How crucial it is to see other cultures, to see how special,
how local they are, how un-universal one's own is.

—Oliver Sacks, *Oaxaca Journal*

"Next year should be my twentieth high school reunion," Mike said.

"Oh, do you want to go?" I asked.

"Maybe," he said. "I wonder how I find out if a reunion is even being organized."

"Typically I think it's organized by whoever was your senior-year class president." I don't know if this is true or not, as I've never been to a class reunion. It's not that I don't want to go, but each reunion that's taken place has occurred at a time when I was either overseas or about to give birth, and the latter condition does not inspire me to visit with long-lost friends. But my guess was that the class president would organize such things. It seems a fair price to pay for having enjoyed an excessive level of popularity during a time when others are experiencing their lifetime peak of acne and awkwardness.

"Shit," Mike said.

"What's wrong?"

"*I* was the senior-year class president."

"Really? How's the reunion planning coming along?"

"I think you know the answer to that question."

"You were class president? So you were Mr. Popular?" This confirmed for me that if Mike and I had attended the same high school, we would not have dated. While he was representing his peers, I was sneaking cigarettes in the girls' bathroom.

"No, I wasn't the most popular, but I pretty much got along with everyone." Another stark contrast between our younger selves. "And it was something I'd always done."

"What do you mean?"

"I ran for class president in the sixth grade, and then I just kept it going every year after that."

"You were class president for seven years in a row?"

"Yep."

"So you were trying to take over the world even back then?"

"I don't know if I'd go that far. Remember, there were only about seventy-five people in my graduating class." Whenever I'm reminded of this, the contrast of our experiences comes to light, and I'm amazed that somehow a girl from Maryland and a boy from Alaska met (in Mexico) and fell in love. We were geographically diverse from the start and perhaps destined to keep the trend going.

Whether or not Mike's class reunion happens (which greatly depends on whether anyone else from his graduating class is willing to step in and take the organizational reins), the possibility was one we instantly expanded on.

"Are you saying you want to go to Alaska?"

"It's been awhile," he confirmed. "And the girls are old

enough now that they might really get into some of the outdoor activities to do there. We could hike, kayak, fish, maybe camp on the beaches." The last time we'd visited Alaska, Emilia was a baby. Mike liked the idea of showing them the place where he grew into the dictator of Sitka High School.

"I wonder if we could make a home exchange out of it."

"I know we could. We'll go in the summer, the best time for weather up there but when all the teachers are dying to escape to the Lower 48 for a bit." As the son of two former teachers for the Sitka school system, Mike has insider knowledge on many Sitka teachers and how they want to spend their summers.

"So, sometime in July or August?"

"Yes," he confirmed.

"Are you sure that's going to work with the schedule of the high school reunion you're not planning?"

"I'll let you know when I get a little further along in the not planning of it."

* * *

There is one question we are asked in regards to vagabonding, to which we never have an answer: "Why did you choose that location?" It's impossible to respond, because we never choose the location. As previously discussed, the location chooses us. It presents itself in the form of a free place to stay at the right time, and we never know exactly when and where that will happen.

During our three months in Mexico, we met and befriended the couple who would later offer us the home in Australia. At the end of our Australian adventure, we made a connection on HomeExchange.com with the family with whom we swapped homes and cars in Brazil.

Sometimes an event or circumstance will lead to a trip, as in the case of turning Mike's possible high school reunion into an Alaskan family adventure. The catalyst for our trip to the Jersey Shore was not an overwhelming craving for deep-fried Twinkies but the result of being offered a free home shortly after someone else offered to rent our home in Boise. We were in Mexico when the offer came in, and while we hadn't planned on leaving Boise so soon after our return, we found it hard to say no to a couple thousand dollars. We accepted the rental without really knowing where we'd go. The next day, my mother and aunt came to visit us in Mexico. When we related our predicament to them, my aunt offered a solution.

"I have a beach house in New Jersey," she said. "You can stay there."

This may not seem unreasonable, the offer of a place to stay for a month from a relative, except for the fact that the day my aunt made this offer was also the first day I'd ever met my aunt. My mother had only known her sister for a few years, having entered the foster care system before my aunt was born. My aunt would also eventually be taken as a ward of the state of Pennsylvania, and both grew up with the knowledge that they had siblings scattered up and down the East Coast. Though they never knew each other as children, and my mother was firmly in her sixties when they met, the two instantly identified as sisters.

"Are you sure you want to make that offer?" I asked. "You know, we do have *kids.*" If my aunt had a second home, a beach house in an affluent neighborhood, there was a chance it would be too nice. What if my kids broke an expensive vase or left sandy, wet butt prints on a white suede couch?

"Of course," my aunt said. "I have all the beach toys you need. The kids will have a blast. You can have the place for the whole month."

My aunt delivered on her generosity, and my fear that my children might wreak havoc was unfounded. *I* was solely responsible for the destruction we caused in the form of a wine stain on the carpet and the accidental bleaching of my aunt's plush and pricey towels.

With the exception of a ten-day trip to Ireland to celebrate our tenth wedding anniversary, we don't choose our locations. We didn't choose Mexico, Vanuatu, Palau, London, Morocco, Brazil, Australia, or the Jersey Shore. But we did consciously make the decision to be open to travel, grateful for it, and to position our lives and careers in such a way that continuous travel is possible.

Moving from a conventional life to vagabonding with kids isn't an automatic switch, but it also isn't one that requires years of planning. Mike and I started with a month-long journey with the specific intent of figuring out what riddles needed to be solved for future, longer trips. Anyone with a similar inclination could do the same. With a commitment to exploring the world without preconceived notions or preju-dice, with an open mind in terms of timing and location, the transition will be easier than you think. There will be trips requiring more effort than others, but rarely will there be a bad one. The world will welcome you with open arms and leave you with no regrets.

* * *

If you enjoyed this book,
please consider posting a review online.

Follow Vagabonding with Kids at

facebook.com/vagabondingwithkids
twitter.com/VagabondingKids
pinterest.com/VagabondKids
instagram.com/vagabondingwithkids

COMING SOON:

Vagabonding with Kids: Australia
Vagabonding with Kids: Brazil
Vagabonding with Kids: Alaska
Vagabonding with Kids: Mexico
Vagabonding with Kids: Thailand

Also by AK Turner

TURN THE PAGE FOR AN EXCERPT
FROM AK TURNER'S NEXT BOOK

Vagabonding with Kids: Australia.

Welcome to Quarantine

A 39-year-old Czech man was selected for a full baggage examination after he arrived on a flight from Dubai. During the examination, ACBPS officers conducted a frisk search of the man and allegedly found 16 small eggs concealed in his groin area.

—Australian Customs and Border Protection Service

Yellow tape designated the quarantine area, a narrow lane in the middle of the floor in which I attempted to keep my family corralled. I'd been quarantined, and they were bringing the drug dog my way. I told myself that the sweat mustache blooming on my upper lip, which has always been one of my more attractive features, had everything to do with the Australian heat permeating the building and worming its way into the Customs and Border Protection area, and nothing to do with the fact that I was being forcibly detained in the Customs and Border Protection area. There was no reason for worry. Illegal wildlife, weapons, and drugs occupied no part of my consciousness, much less my baggage, groin, or body cavity. Still, I continued to sweat, and the dog approached.

Twenty-four hours earlier, I stood in an airport in Idaho and thought, *I want to be married to the man doing lunges in the airport.* And luckily, I was. I watched as Mike instructed five-year-old Ivy on the proper posture of the perfect lunge. The image, endearing to me, could only have startled a stranger: there was my husband, a grown man lunging in a public area not typically suited for exercise, mirrored by a ponytailed child clad in leggings, a rainbow tutu, and a shirt with a giant unicorn on the front.

"Like this, Daddy?"

"Yep," he answered. "Feel the burn."

I didn't join in on the lunging but later led a rousing game of Simon Says before Mike and I had the girls run ten laps around a large bank of seats, warning them to give other travelers a wide berth as they did so. Looking up to find an unknown child charging you in a maelstrom of pink and unicorns can be alarming, and I didn't want to be held responsible for the early death by heart attack of an unsuspecting business traveler.

Simon said all he had to say, and we couldn't force them to run any more laps, unless we wanted cruelty added to our list of parenting skills. Boredom commenced. The fact that we were dealing with the B word a mere hour into a twenty-four-hour trip was troublesome but undeniable. I knew it had taken hold when Emilia ratted out her little sister. "Mom, Ivy's licking the wall again."

"Ivy, please stop licking things." This is a command I speak more often than I care to admit. "Hey, I have a great idea!"

"What is it?" Emilia asked, her eyes wide with anticipation.

"Let's go to the *bathroom!*"

"Yeah!" They cheered and jumped with joy. This is contrary to the reaction I get when asking them to use the bathroom before leaving home. Public restrooms, however, are always a treat. Porta-Potties are especially revered, leading me to wonder if they share a faulty sense of smell.

Ivy and I took the handicapped stall while Emilia, eager to show her independence and maturity at the age of seven, went solo in the stall next to us. As soon as she was settled into what was apparently a much-needed urination, Ivy reached over and stuck her hand in the sanitary napkin depository. "What's this, Mama?"

"Don't touch that!" She withdrew her hand, and the metal lid closed with a creak. I heard an identical creak from the stall next to us as Emilia apparently withdrew *her* hand from her sanitary napkin depository, as well. I didn't bother explaining the receptacle's purpose. We'd been through the conversation many times before, and it hadn't done any good, because that odd little box on the wall just beckons. It's so intriguing. To them, it's one of the many perks found in a public restroom. This would not be the last time their hands acted on curiosity in an airport facility. Luckily, my children are as enamored with the sinks and soaps of public bathrooms as they are with the hidden treasures of the toilet stalls.

I waited until we exited the restroom to take a deep breath, visualizing myself inhaling excitement and exhaling fear. This is the type of action that I do often but that if anyone told me to do would immediately cause me to roll my eyes. I employ a variety of meditative tools, to which I would never admit, when we embark on months-long journeys to other countries. These quell the panic of the other me, who is a creature of habit and most comfortable when following a schedule so monotonous and predictable that it would make normal people opt instead to chew off their own feet.

When people ask why we travel for months at a time, the logical answer always seems to be because we can. In that regard, I have a lot in common with mountain climbers, who profess to climb mountains because the mountains are there. Actually that's a ridiculous lie, and there's no truth in the Everest analogy, because I'd keel over halfway to base camp. Either that or I'd bitch about the cold so much that one of my companion climbers would give me a well-timed nudge over a cliff, which I'd surely deserve. Nonetheless, we travel because the world is there, and we'd rather live in a place for months at a time than vacation there for a week. We're drawn to the challenge and intrigued by the logistical puzzle of living and working in another country. And anyone lucky enough to have the blessing-curse hybrid of self-employment might as well take advantage of the perk of mobility.

One hour and half a bottle of hand sanitizer later, we were on the flight to LAX when I realized that Ivy was a quarter of the way through one of the workbooks I'd purchased for her. One of the few materials that was supposed to last us months, and we weren't yet out of the country. Well, obviously my child is gifted, I reasoned, but I wanted to make it last, so we put the workbook away and replaced it with BrainQuest cards. These are flashcards, of sorts. They have pictures and require reasoning and deduction to get the correct answer. Some are more difficult than others. She whizzed through half the deck, again confirming my suspicions of her innate intelligence.

On a previous trip abroad, we'd enrolled both girls in a Montessori school, but the amount of moving around we'd undertake within Australia prohibited the possibility of them regularly attending a school. In planning the trip, Mike used the H word tentatively at first. As we discussed it, I often found that I couldn't say it without stuttering, so that it always came out as huh-homeschooling, as if I required a syllable of exhale before I could bring myself to utter the word in its entirety. I'd come to accept that I would (huh) homeschool the children, using a mix of materials, including those given to us by their teachers, online programs, workbooks, and a few supplemental fun activities, like the BrainQuest cards. I flipped the next card and read the question. "What part of your body should you wash before you eat a meal?"

"Your body?"

"No, Ivy. What *part* of your body?"

"Your teeth?"

"Ivy, what do we wash before we eat a meal?"

"Your head?"

The entire plane was learning that we were a filthy, disgusting family. Not only did my girls explore the sanitary napkin bin, but they also didn't know what to wash before eating.

"Ivy," I took on a stern tone, as if that would somehow get her to say the correct answer. "What part of your body do you wash before you eat?"

"Your arms?" She said this loudly. Her increased volume was an answer to the increase in the severity of my tone. Either that or she wanted to make sure the entire plane heard.

"What do we do after we go potty?" I whispered. I thought maybe I could save face by getting her to say the correct answer, even if I had to cheat a little bit and alter the question.

"Wipe our private parts?" she boomed.

"Wash your *hands*, Ivy. You should always wash your hands before you eat a meal."

"Oh." She looked confused, as if this was the first time she'd ever heard such a ridiculous idea.

"I'll tell you what, Ivy. Let's put the BrainQuest cards away for a while. Do you want to play Would You Rather?"

"Okay," she answered. "I'll go first. Would you rather marry Daddy or have cake?"

"Ooh, that's a tough one." I *was* hungry. But again, my husband was the man not afraid to do lunges in the middle of an airport. And he was within earshot. "I'd rather marry Daddy." We continued on with Would You Rather, with each of Ivy's questions to me involving some sort of confection, forcing me to choose between different forms of sugar. She posed the scenarios with desperation in her voice, as if nothing could be more heart wrenching than deciding on cake versus cupcake. Pitting cookie against brownie might as well have been *Sophie's Choice*.

The conversation struck me as sweet in more ways than one. When I flew as a child, the only topic I can remember talking about with my mother was death. We would weigh the odds of our plane crashing and joke about the improbability of a successful water landing, because let's be honest, if you crash in the ocean, you're not really going to slide down the ramp and board a little raft until safety arrives. Our morbid subject material wasn't relegated only to air travel. To this day, even with our feet firmly planted on the ground, conversations with my mother often turn to serial killers, unsolved murders, and other violent topics, which we are inexplicably compelled to share with each other. I can only hope for a similarly tender relationship with my own daughters as they mature.

Ivy and I weren't yet at that stage, though I often saw hints of it when she'd ask the questions, "Mom, when you die, will your hair still be there?" and "Mom, what would happen if a person touched fire to their eyeball?" For the flight, though, she was content to remain in the realm of sugar until we landed, presenting me with such difficult choices as, "Would

you rather have a cake with pink frosting and purple sprinkles or purple frosting and pink sprinkles?" Oh, the dilemma.

At LAX, my least favorite airport on the planet but one
in which I frequently find myself, Emilia remarked, "Lots of
people here have brown skin." Statements like these reinforce
my desire to travel with my children as much as possible. Life
in Idaho can be blindingly white, though thankfully offset by
Boise's emergence as a hub for refugees. As much as I love
Idaho, I'm determined to show my daughters that the world
is full of different people and cultures and thinking. And that
all of those things are beautiful.

But perhaps LAX is not the best place to focus on such
teaching moments. Because in the crush of harried travelers and high tensions, it's hard to look past the fact that it's
just a big, loud, overcrowded, overpriced, and difficult-to-
navigate airport full of ornery people and a pervasive lack of
logic. And anyone who works at LAX should receive hazard
pay for having to survive in such an environment. Or maybe
one Xanax per shift.

We exited security, picked up our luggage, rechecked
our luggage, and headed for security. The inefficiency of this
process made me feel many things, not one of which was
secure. The routine makes my heart race. I'm not afraid of
the body scan or having every square inch of my luggage
searched. It's a panic that I will inexplicably blurt out the
word *bomb*, simply because I'm not supposed to. There's also
the fear that in the rush of passengers removing belts and
shoes and compulsively checking their boarding passes, I will
lose something really important, like a child. Or a *computer*.
Mike and I often look to our laptops as members of the family.
There is a constant need to verify their proximity and health,

because working overseas for months at a time only works if we are able to work. I passed through without being mistakenly identified as a terrorist, and in possession of one husband, two children, and my laptop.

By the time we took off for Brisbane, I wanted nothing more than to sleep. Ivy snuggled with heavy eyelids into her blankie, while Emilia fell asleep using the armrest as an awkward pillow. As she sank deeper into sleep, gravity took hold, and her lower jaw dropped down, while her top teeth remained caught, so that after a few minutes, her mouth was fully around the armrest, giving the impression that she was gnawing on something in her dreams. Her position amused but also disturbed me, as I viewed it even more unsanitary than sticking your hand in the sanitary napkin disposal box.

I looked across my daughters to Mike, who sat with his eyes serenely closed. My family was asleep. We had a fourteen-hour flight ahead of us. It was the perfect time for rest, and I needed sleep. But this was trumped by a shooting pain in my leg, which I was sure was a blood clot that would kill me. I was as sure of the blood clot as I had been when a swollen gland was lymphoma, which, of course, was really just a swollen gland, or when I had chronic jaw pain that was clear evidence of a tumor. And when I say chronic, I mean every so often for two and a half weeks. I mean, what constitutes chronic, really? But the bright side of the blood clot, if that was to be the cause of my demise, was that it would be much better than the other possibility of the plane going down. At least my family would be spared. Yes, good news indeed.

Qantas Airlines seemed like a safe bet. Australians are forced to innovate when it comes to travel, because when your country also occupies your continent, you have to get more adventurous than an extended road trip if you're going to venture internationally. And when you're surrounded by a number of oceans and seas, perhaps you dedicate a little extra thought to how best to cross them. Australians invented both the black box flight recorder and the inflatable escape slide, one of which implied a quest for truth in the face of tragedy, while the other seemed evidence of an inherently Australian optimism in the face of crashing into the ocean. I admired both perspectives.

While waiting for the blood clot to kill me, I settled in to make the best of my situation. I'd always thought Qantas would be luxurious. International flights, excluding short stints from the United States to Mexico, were supposed to carry with them a good deal of pampering, which is necessary to get otherwise rational humans through a fourteen-hour flight. But the Qantas flight had the same cramped discomfort that I associated with domestic flights. Sure, airlines had to cut costs, and airline travel no longer held the same exotic appeal that it once had, but still. To offer me alcohol only once during a fourteen-hour flight? What sort of cruelty was this? And why did the seats feel as tiny as those on a crappy little commuter plane? Had they been downsized too? A frightening but very real possibility struck me. What if the seats were the same size as they'd always been on international flights, but my ass was a few sizes bigger than the last time I'd traveled? The distance from my body to the back of the seat in front of me was also probably the same but seemed smaller now that my protruding belly required an additional allotment of this very precious real estate. And I wasn't even pregnant.

Other distances to contemplate were less distressing and far more interesting. Our plane would travel 11,575 kilometers from Los Angeles to Brisbane. I knew this because our flight data was plastered on the screen, which, because the occupant of the seat in front of me had reclined, was a mere two inches from my face. Along with 11,575 kilometers across the Pacific Ocean came the element of time travel. We left the United States on a Sunday night and after the fourteen-hour flight would arrive in Brisbane on Tuesday morning, leaving the Monday in the interim lost in time. It simply would not exist for us, though if you have to lose one day of the week, I guess Monday would be the one to go. We would regain this time, of course, on the way back, when we'd depart Australia on a Tuesday morning, and after twenty hours of flying on four different planes, and six hours of layovers in three different airports (one of which was sadly LAX), we'd arrive to find it only Tuesday afternoon.

Emilia stirred next to me, dislodged her jaw from the armrest, and sat up. I wanted to share with her the magnitude of these facts.

"Emilia, do you realize that we're traveling 11,575 kilometers?" I pointed to the data on the screen in front of me.

"Wow," she said, nearly punching me in the face as she stretched. "That's a lot. I think I need to write that down for part of my homework." I retrieved a homework folder with questions for her to answer on the plane. "How many miles are we traveling?" she asked.

"I'm not sure how many miles, but it's 11,575 kilometers. Isn't that amazing?"

"Yes, but how many *miles* is it?"

"It's thousands!" I was trying to maintain the sense of wonder but felt failure creeping in. I've never been good at converting things, from units of measurement to the convertible bra.

Emilia sighed. "That doesn't really help me, Mom."

The following day, I would look it up and give her the number 7,192. This would be the first of many disappointing instances of completing homework in which I employed Google and fed her the answer.

Emilia and Ivy passed the time in a rotation of eating, sleeping, and watching movies. The presence of individual televisions on international flights makes them oddly more bearable than shorter, domestic flights, and it's a wonder that I felt any discomfort, given that eating, sleeping, and watching movies are three of my favorite pastimes.

Hours later, as we began our descent into Brisbane, the flight attendant made an announcement that no food would be permitted through customs. Not even food from the airplane. My girls each had a purse. One was pink with a rainbow of sequins, the other pink with *My Little Pony*. Both were chockfull of various airplane snacks that I'd been hoarding away over the last twenty hours. I'm compelled to save every ration of pretzels and peanuts, because I feel it's my right after spending thousands of dollars on airfare. I want my rightful snacks, whether I consume them or not.

The plane landed safely, at which point I had to admit to myself that our Australian adventure was actually going to happen. The blood clot didn't make it to my brain or my heart or wherever it needed to go to kill me, and the biggest failures of the flight were my inability to convert kilometers to miles and the crew's failure to offer me more than one alcoholic beverage. Mechanical failure wasn't even in the running, despite the fact that I'd spent the previous six months vacillating between excitement and certainty that the plane would go down. Neither the black box flight recorder nor the inflatable escape slide would be needed.

"Mom, can I have the Kit Kat now?" Emilia asked.

"Not right now, sweetie." Two tiny Kit Kat bars were part of the hoarded stash of food, but I had to put my go face on and wrangle luggage and children. I wasn't equipped to deal with chocolate-covered children. "We'll have them later."

We disembarked and walked down a long corridor, dotted with signs on how food was not allowed through customs. These signs were placed over trash cans, encouraging travelers to dispose of any food items they might be carrying. But how could I throw away perfectly good food? That seemed unnatural. So I continued on. But then I hesitated. I am innately a rule follower.

"Mike, do you think I should ditch this stuff?" I motioned to one of the girls' purses, brimming with an assortment of wrapped goodies.

"Now can I have the Kit Kat?" Emilia asked.

"No," I answered.

"It's fine," Mike said offhandedly.

I chided myself. We got in line for immigration, where a man approached me and asked to see my customs form. "Do you have any food?" he asked.

"Uh."

"Just tell me now."

"Just some stuff from the plane," I fessed and flashed him one of the cereal bars from the *My Little Pony* purse. He waved us on, and I relaxed.

"Mom, I have to pee," said Emilia.

"Well, you'll just have to wait."

It occurred to me then that while Mike had taken Ivy to the bathroom twice on the plane, because he's one of those phenomenal husbands who doesn't push every distasteful task onto his wife, Emilia hadn't used the bathroom once during the entire flight. Which was great, because no one actually enjoys using a bathroom on a plane, even my Porta-Potty-loving kids. But Emilia hadn't peed in about sixteen hours. Was that normal? Had I subconsciously dehydrated my own child to avoid taking her to the airplane bathroom?

"I can wait," she said, and I thought that she must have inherited her dad's bladder capabilities, as Mike urinates twice daily while I go about every forty-five minutes, not including involuntary urination, which happens whenever I sneeze. "But now can I have the Kit Kat?"

"No, Emilia." I really wanted her to shut up about the Kit Kat. I pictured myself doing time in an Australian prison for attempting to smuggle a Kit Kat into the country.

After immigration, we retrieved our substantial luggage and, with form in hand, entered a line to go through customs. And I should have known better. Because whenever you travel for more than ten days, you get the full search. We would be in Australia for months.

Before I knew it, there I was in the quarantine line. And the drug dog was heading my way. Staring at me as if to say, *I can smell those chocolate-covered wafers you're hiding. I know about the salted nuts.* My sweat mustache bloomed again in all its glory. I was going to end up in jail over a Kit Kat. And not even one that I would get to eat. And not even a full-sized candy bar. This thing was pathetically small, smaller even than Halloween candy. The dog inched closer and then moved past the *My Little Pony* purse without a moment's hesitation.

My heart pounded. *I got away with it,* I thought. *I'm an international smuggler.* Sure, it's not like I had four pounds of hashish strapped to my body, but still. Then the dog sat down. Her handler took hold of the other purse; the rainbow of sequins apparently failed to portray innocence. The handler opened it and rifled through the cereal bars and pretzels, seeming not to care about them at all. I felt relief again. These minor snacks didn't matter. I had been worrying over nothing. Until her hand withdrew from the purse a shiny red apple. And she looked at me as if condemning Eve for her transgression. Mike looked at me with the same disdain, a look that said, "Do I even know you?"

That's when shit got serious. Every inch of luggage was searched. The apple was confiscated and placed in a plastic bag. We were handed over to the care of a new customs officer. I'd filled out the customs forms. I'd packed the bags. I claimed responsibility. And only for a second did I contemplate throwing one of my children under the bus. Because surely they wouldn't send a child to do time for the apple.

"You have violated Australian Quarantine Law. We could fine you. We could give you up to ten years in prison." He paused for effect.

I almost blurted, "But it's an apple!" but didn't want to suffer the spiel of the potential harm of my environmental violation.

"But none of that will happen today. Instead we're going to give you a warning." On a photocopied paper that detailed the penalties I could have faced, he wrote my name. Even my middle name, which made it seem extra serious.

When we made it through, I was furious with myself for not listening to my instincts and throwing away all of the snacks when I had the chance. I'd wanted to, but I also wanted to be the type of person who was relaxed and casual and moved about the world without constantly worrying about trivialities. And it's these two warring desires that screw me.

"See," I said to Mike. "This is why I'm a rule follower. I should have just ditched everything. But you told me not to worry about it." I burned with humiliation, fumed like a child caught cheating.

"Yeah," he said, "but I didn't know you had an *apple.*"

"It's not like it was a poisoned apple!"

"You can't mess around with fruit. They take that *very* seriously."

As much as I wanted to be angry with Mike, I was angry with myself. I'd failed. And yet we were free to go, embarking on a monumental journey. We were officially Down Under. And a small part of me felt like an international ninja smuggler, because there was still that matter of the Kit Kat. And *that* fucker made it through.

* * *

Australian Disco

*Of the 828 bird species listed in Australia,
about half are found nowhere else.*

—Tourism Australia

Our first morning in Australia, we were wakened at 4:30 a.m. by a swelling cacophony. It began with chirps and delicate tweets. A laser-like birdcall chimed in, and I felt I'd fallen inside of a giant video game. The laser was the call of the eastern whipbird, not to be confused with the lyrebird, which makes an entirely different laser-like sound, also reminiscent of a video game but perhaps from a different weapon. The kookaburra joined in next, which I would have sworn was a monkey. By the time I was fully conscious, I had the odd image in my head of a troop of primates, geared in helmets and elbow pads, creeping in the jungle outside our bedroom window, engaged in an epic battle of laser tag. *The Planet of the Apes* image persisted, despite the fact that I was on the only continent that has rain forests but no monkeys. Against all logic, I peered out of the windows to search for them. Not only did I fail to see laser-wielding monkeys, but I also didn't see any of the birds responsible for the noise. The view was of a thick jungle, in which one towering tree couldn't be distinguished from the next, a riot of green in vines, stalks, fronds, and ferns.

We had arrived the day earlier to a hilltop home on the edge of a rain forest on the Sunshine Coast. We exited a shuttle and hiked a steep driveway. The air was dense and humid, and we breathed heavily, dragging our luggage (minus one confiscated apple and two devoured Kit Kats) and children. Approaching the front door signified the merciful end to our twenty-four hours of travel from Idaho.

A long-limbed, sleek woman opened the door.

"Hello!" I smiled. "We made it."

"Yes." She smiled back before a poorly masked shade of fear swept her face. "Oh, you have little ones." Her body blocked the doorway, as if physically conveying that she had changed her mind, that we would not be allowed entry, that she was turning us away and we'd better run down her impossibly steep driveway, begin flailing our arms to hail our shuttle, and start the long journey back to Boise.

"Yes," I confirmed, looking down at my not-so-little little one. "This is Ivy." I wanted to add: *She is one of my two children, whose existence and ages were disclosed to you ten months ago when we began discussing this arrangement.* But I didn't.

"Well," she tried to recover her smile and resigned herself to the inevitable, "come in."

Our host was both an artist and art collector and possessed the type of grace that made the term *artist* too pedestrian for her. *Artiste* made more sense. Her home was ours for four weeks, in a complex system of home exchanges. She took us on a tour of the house, in which everything was either white or made of glass, save for bright red paintings, precarious sculptures, and a grand piano.

"Ooh, Mom, can I play the piano?" Emilia asked.

"No." I shot a look at her that said, *Please be silent and still until the Artiste leaves.* Emilia did not get the message.

"This," the homeowner said, gesturing to the piano, "is a family treasure." My daughters' eyes lit up at the mention of treasure. This would make them want to touch it more. "And I ask that you not set anything on it, aside from papers."

Mental note: *Don't touch the family jewels. Don't set anything on it, even paper. Convince kids there is no treasure hidden inside the piano.*

One of the bedrooms had two children's beds, but I still had the impression that the Artiste was not at ease among children and could only assume the bedroom existed for the occasional and likely brief visits of grandchildren.

The master bathroom was home to a giant soaker tub.

"Ooh, look at the bathtub!" Ivy squealed.

"Please don't use this tub," instructed the homeowner. "It uses too much water, and water here is so very scarce."

She spoke in earnest as someone who felt a deep connection to the land, someone who had felt the plague of drought and ached in her heart because of it. I promised that we would be conscientious of our use of water, and I meant it. We'd take quick showers, and our children would bathe in the smaller tub with minimal water. I'd subdue my passion for sterility to preserve this precious resource. I would *not* be a wasteful, inconsiderate tourist.

We followed her into the living room. "As you can see, everything here is just so dry." Her voice still had the pain of one who had long tried to farm drought-stricken land. And as she spoke, she gestured out to her magnificent view, which showed an endless expanse of the lushest, thickest, greenest rain forest I'd ever seen.

The tour continued outside where she introduced me to two-dozen potted plants tucked underneath her deck, which I was to water twice a week. Another mental note: *Conserve water at all costs. Except when it comes to potted plants hidden under the deck.*

Eventually there was nothing left to show us, so she handed over the keys and left, which I'm sure pained her. Home exchanges sound wonderful until you relinquish your dwelling, with all of its treasures and your accumulated possessions, to strangers. I didn't fault her for her obvious discomfort but felt relief when she finally departed. And then Ivy began fondling a statue of a bare-breasted woman, poking at the nipples and inserting her hand in the cleavage. I silently thanked her for waiting until the Artiste had gone. In the coming weeks, Ivy would create a ritual of fondling the statue, grasping a breast with each passing.

When we'd settled in and properly molested the artwork, Mike called one of his friends from college who, as fate would have it, lived in Australia with his wife and two children, not far from our accommodations in Queensland. Levi is a ship's pilot in Alaska, bringing foreign vessels into Yakutat, Ketchikan, Glacier Bay, and Sitka, among other harbors, a job that allows him to work only part of the year and live and play anywhere else in the world the rest of the time. We hadn't seen him in over a decade and were excited about the reunion. When he arrived that afternoon, we found that he hadn't changed much in the previous ten years, other than having acquired the roles of husband and father, at which he excelled. From Mike's college days, I remembered Levi as exceedingly kind and optimistic, the type of person for whom every expression is some version of a smile.

"So good to see you guys!" he gushed upon arrival. "Do you have a car? Do you want one of ours?" When a friend you haven't seen in years hands his car over to you, asking for nothing in return, you know he's a keeper.

Levi drove us to his home in Coolum where we visited with his family. Our daughters discussed their favorite *My Little Pony* pony while the adults chatted over a beer. "Should we walk down to the beach?" Levi suggested. "It's just a short walk, and there's a playground for the kids."

Short is relative. If you're talking about distances comparative to a marathon, then I would concede that two miles is short. But when you add a five-year-old who thinks that tutus and sparkly shoes are good hiking gear, two miles is torturous, for the parents more than the child.

Along the way, we stopped to observe a tree brimming with fruit bats, and I marveled every time great white cockatoos swept overhead. The vision of cockatoos flying free caused me to waver between a desire to return to vegetarianism as a show of solidarity with all living creatures, versus my competing desire to try a meat pie from a fast-food joint we'd passed called Beefy's.

When we reached the playground, the kids showed off their climbing skills while the adults gazed out at the ocean.

"So, just how likely are we to die here?" I asked. I was joking. Mostly.

Levi laughed and proceeded to educate me about Surf Life Saving Australia, a volunteer organization that serves as lifeguards, monitors shark activity, and wears adorable little beanies, all of which convinced me that my family might actually survive the trip.

"But *how* do they monitor shark activity?" I asked.

"They have shark nets set up."

"Nets?"

"Well, they're not actual nets, but it's called a shark net. There are baited buoys, and they monitor the bait."

"Wait, so they're *baiting* the sharks into the beach?" Maybe survival wasn't probable, after all.

"Don't worry, Amanda. They're monitored way offshore, they have helicopter patrols, and you're going to be just fine."

"Okay," I said, while silently wondering how I could keep my family from going in the water.

"Mom," Emilia interrupted. "Can we go in the water?"

"We will another time, Emilia. I promise. But not today, because we don't have our swimsuits."

"Okay, Mom," she said, at which point both Emilia and Ivy hiked up their skirts and went in anyway. I didn't protest, which was my way of acknowledging that passing on my disproportionate fear of water to my daughters would be less than responsible parenting.

Before we departed that day, Levi and his wife invited us to return in a week for Thanksgiving dinner.

"That would be great," I said. Thanksgiving is easily my favorite holiday, because it requires no decorations and presents while still allowing me to gorge on food and drink. And because we were in Australia through the fall and winter, I'd assumed I'd miss out on the gluttony of the season altogether. "What would you like me to make?" I asked.

"Amanda can make *anything*," Mike said. I blushed at my husband's confidence in me but also silently recognized that my culinary skills don't translate well in foreign kitchens with unfamiliar ingredients. It was decided that I'd contribute a casserole and a pumpkin pie, which were well within my capabilities.

With our plans of overindulgence in place, Levi's wife handed over the keys to her Subaru for us to borrow for the next week or so. Our kids climbed in the backseat while Mike and I clumsily approached the wrong sides of the vehicle before realizing our error, as well as the fact that this wasn't likely to inspire Levi's confidence in us. I walked back around to the left side of the vehicle and felt odd sitting with no steering wheel in front of me. Mike sat in the driver's seat and placed his left hand on the stick shift.

"You can do this," I said.

"I know I can do this. I'm not worried."

"Okay, good. Because you shouldn't be. And don't worry about the fact that they're standing there watching us and that you have to back out of this extremely long and narrow driveway."

"I love you," Mike said, "but I'm going to have to ask that you stop speaking."

We waved meekly at Levi and his wife and slowly made our getaway. I clenched my teeth in anticipation of the crunch of metal, which thankfully never came.

Driving required Mike to display his freakishly competent skills at navigating a car on the left side of the road, with the driver's seat on the right side of the car. And because the car was a stick shift, he shifted with his left hand, so that first gear was away from the body. Trying to comprehend all of this hurt my brain and made me constantly question the concepts of left and right. Mike managed with little problem, though for the first few days I heeded Levi's advice by repeating the steady reminder of "Keep left, keep left, keep left." I thought it was nice of Australia to accommodate foreigners with the Keep Left signs dotting the highway.

As we drove between beach towns on the Sunshine Coast, I scanned the landscape for wildlife, hoping for my sake as well as my children's that the first kangaroo we saw wouldn't be roadkill. I was sure that every tree was home to a koala that wanted to crawl down and cuddle with me. Though the wildlife didn't make itself known on that first afternoon, we did drive by magnificent flame trees and brilliant purple jacarandas, giving the landscape the appearance of a green, orange, and violet Pollock canvas.

With our borrowed car and finagled home, I felt pretty comfortable about settling in for our journey. As our first full day in Australia came to a close, Mike and I sat down with a glass of wine. Everything felt in place and as it should be.

"We made it," I said with a smile.

"I'm freaking out," said Mike.

"What? What are you talking about?" I'd had such a feeling of ease a moment before. For Mike to be freaking out, there had to be something I didn't know. Did he have a secret gambling addiction, and loan shark thugs were tracking us down? Had he been running a Ponzi scheme, and the feds were closing in? Was that why he'd been so amenable to leaving the country? Or was it another woman? Could I anticipate a *Fatal Attraction* psycho sneaking into our borrowed home? I would take that bitch *down!*

"We don't have any plan for what we're going to do after we leave this house," Mike said. "We don't know where we're going to live for the second half of the trip."

"Yes, but we just got here. This is day one."

"I know."

"For the past six months, every time I tried to plan the rest of the trip, you told me to relax."

"Because you were freaking out," he said.

"But I was only freaking out so that we'd have everything in place and could avoid *this*. I wanted to avoid a freak-out during the trip."

"Maybe we just have different ideas about when it's the appropriate time to freak out," he reasoned. "In any case, we're here, and I'm panicking because we don't have anything figured out."

"Stay calm," I commanded. "You're not having a regular freak-out."

"I'm not?"

"No. You're having the *traveler* freak-out."

"I am?"

"Yes. I know what you're feeling. It happened to me when we were in Mexico for three months. Remember?"

"Yeah." He nodded. "But you were questioning the meaning of life and stuff."

"The traveler freak-out comes in many different forms."

It's true, and a condition well known to part-time digital nomads like ourselves. Emotions run high, and panic sets in, bringing with it all manner of questions, including what the hell are we doing here, what is the meaning of life, how can we possibly afford this, and how *does* sand manage to get its way into the bed despite all of my efforts to the contrary.

To remedy the freak-out, we spent days making plans for the rest of the trip. This involved dozens of phone calls during which we learned that hotels and rental units were booked.

We are never as original as we suppose, and the idea of escaping winter by traveling to summer on the other side of the world was not solely ours. The lack of available accommodations intensified Mike's stress level. We'd relax every time we had another piece of the itinerary puzzle in place, then add more debt to our credit card to secure our reservations, which spawned an entirely new avenue for freak-outs.

In planning the rest of the trip, we knew we wanted to head south to Tasmania, and we also wanted to see more of Australia along the way, so we decided to book a small RV, travel down the coast for a few weeks, and then stay in a few places in Tasmania. In reality, we didn't so much *decide* where to stay in Tasmania as book anything that was available.

As we looked at places to camp along the coast of the mainland, we viewed websites for dozens of campgrounds with events for kids.

"Ooh, look at this place," Mike said. "They have an event called Kids' Disco and Karate!"

"Wow, that's ambitious." I tried to wrap my head around it. Did they incorporate karate moves into dance? Did you learn how to break a cinder block while doing the hustle? "Australian disco must be really awesome, being the home of ABBA."

"Tell me you didn't just say that," Mike scowled.

"ABBA? Not Australian?"

"Swedish."

"Oh, right. I was thinking of the Bee Gees."

My husband looked at me as if I'd punched him in the gut. "What?"

"British."

"Right. Okay, so maybe Australian disco isn't really a thing. I still don't understand Kids' Disco and Karate." I pictured a four-year-old in a tiny karate gi and headband, dancing to "I'm Your Boogie Man" under a disco ball. Whenever I fail to connect a phrase in my head, I remind myself to stop and consider the source. I looked at what Mike was reading.

"You mean Kids' Disco and *Karaoke*," I corrected.

"Oh." He looked disappointed. "Kids' Disco and Karate sounded so much cooler."

We finalized our camping itinerary (sadly without the inclusion of disco, karaoke, or karate) down the east coast of Australia, and I wondered how we'd make the transition going from the opulence of our borrowed home in Queensland to living in a souped-up van with two kids. The thought made me claustrophobic.

Once we had a plan in place for the rest of our travels, Mike calmed down, and we settled into enjoying our surroundings, searching out places and activities that were distinctly Australian and ignoring the American culture that seemed to be everywhere. McDonald's is as pervasive as religion throughout the world, which makes me feel oddly ashamed, but beyond that, we saw T-shirts advertising UFC or branded with US locations like Brooklyn, Indianapolis, and California. Billboards pushed Coke in a rainbow of cans, and we encountered the usual suspects of Starbucks and 7-11 and Walmart. Perhaps the most depressing American encroachment was Sizzler. You just don't want to fly to the other side of the world and see a Sizzler. At least I don't. As a result, I would gravitate toward anything that gave the impression of being inherently Australian, which often incorporated an air of relaxed friendliness and an appreciation for the landscape itself.

After two days, my awe and appreciation of the rain forest outside of our bedroom window was tempered by my desire to shoot the birds. I recognized my human arrogance and the fact that the birds' presence was far more natural than my own, so instead I instituted the habit of waking at four in the morning to shut the windows, which we left open at night in the hopes that cool air would work its way inside, before the cacophony reached its crescendo. At least the birds were outside. Inside, we'd dispatched a fair number of insects and one giant arachnid, which thankfully my girls did not see. They did, however, witness a few cockroach encounters.

I stood in the hallway one evening as they sat on the couch in the living room.

"It's time to get ready for bed, girls."

"What?!" Emilia said indignantly, as if I don't utter these same words at the same time every evening of her life.

"Come on. Let's brush teeth and go potty."

Ivy sulked as if I'd asked her to learn Latin, but both girls trudged my way.

"Wait," I snapped. "Hold on just a second."

A light brown roach perched on the wall next to me, and I wanted to dispose of it while they were still at arm's length.

"What's wrong?" Emilia asked.

"Oh, nothing," I answered. "Hand me the newspaper on the coffee table, would you?"

She did so, then, seeing the bug, took another step back.

"It's okay, just a little insect. I'll take care of it." I was trying to sound casual. I didn't want my daughters to gain an unnatural fear of bugs. But my casual tone infected my actions, and when I swatted at the roach, it was more lackadaisical than I'd intended. As soon as I failed to hit the bug, the roach demonstrated that it had wings. It flew directly from the wall to my bare calf and sprinted up my dress. I began a frantic, high-stepping hop, all while trying to keep my face placid for the benefit of my kids, the combination of which somehow caused me to drool on my own breasts.

"Mom, are you okay?" Ivy asked.

"I'm fine," I said calmly, while stomping as hard as I could in an effort to dislodge the roach from my thigh. "I just didn't expect that sucker to fly." The bug hit the floor, and I crushed it with my flip-flop over and over again.

"Mom," Emilia said. "I think it's dead."

"Yes," I said, out of breath and flushed. "Nothing to worry about."

I'm not sure why having a roach on my body is so terrifying. It's not going to bite me or sting me, and if it defecates on me, the resultant matter will be microscopic, and I won't ever know about it. But there's the lurking fear that one day I will encounter a roach that intends to burrow into my body and begin colonizing there, so I was unable to react in any way other than hopping around in a move that I came to think of as the Australian disco.

* * *

Acknowledgements

Thanks to Ross Patty, Merilee Marsh, Ellen Morfit, Ruth Knox, Stacy Ennis, Christy Hovey, Elaine Ambrose, Jen Mann, and Chris Day for their time, encouragement, and keen eyes.

I cannot imagine completing a project like this without the immeasurable talents of Sarah Tregay and Elizabeth Day.

Thanks to my in-laws for their tolerance.

Thanks to my daughter Emilia for keeping us safe with her survival knowledge.

Thanks to my daughter Ivy for making sure we don't forget the snacks.

And thanks to Mike for the adventure. For everything.